THE GREAT WESTERN RAILWAY

HOW IT GREW

KEN GIBBS

AMBERLEY

*To the memory of all those who, now long gone, by their endeavours,
directly or indirectly, turned an idea into the icon known today as*
THE GREAT WESTERN RAILWAY

Front cover image © Colin G. Maggs

First published 2012

Amberley Publishing
The Hill, Stroud
Gloucestershire, GL5 4EP

www.amberleybooks.com

British Library Cataloguing in Publication Data.
A catalogue record for this book is available from the British Library.

ISBN 978 1 4456 0450 3

Typeset in 10pt on 12pt Sabon.
Typesetting and Origination by Amberley Publishing.
Printed in the UK.

Contents

THE Gentlemen deputed by the Corporation, the Society of Merchant Venturers, the Dock Company, the Chamber of Commerce, and the Bristol and Gloucestershire Rail Road Company, to take into consideration the expediency of promoting the formation of a RAIL ROAD from BRISTOL to LONDON, request you to favor them, in writing, with such information as you may be able to afford, respecting the expediency of the proposed Rail Road, addressed to the CHAIRMAN, in time to be laid before an adjourned Meeting of the said Deputies, to be held at the COUNCIL-HOUSE, on THURSDAY, the 31st Instant, at Twelve o'Clock.

I am, &c.

JOHN CAVE,

Chairman

BRISTOL, 21st Jan. 1833.

Notice of proposal.

Introduction

The Great Western Railway (GWR) has always been with us, or so it may seem from the books and memories which abound. We tend to think of the huge triangle, its points on London, Birkenhead and the tip of Cornwall, covering much of the South West and Wales as 'Great Western' territory. It was not always thus!

People have migrated and wandered from the dawn of history. All have left their mark: the tracks and bridleways, the roads of the Romans, and the drovers' roads, and pack horse trails that crisscross the country. Their legacies dot the villages. How many 'Drove Roads' exist, and how many hamlets sport a 'Pack Horse' bridge? How many urban areas have a 'Wharf Road', with houses all around and no sign of a canal? Communities settled and expanded. Agricultural and populace centres developed and for all of this expansion the transport was the horse and inevitable cart. The roads became busier; clouds of dust in summer and impassable mud in winter. Boats plied the stretches of river that were navigable, many rivers winding their way to the sea and thus taking the developing communities along their courses, finishing at the coast and allowing a flourishing coastal traffic by water to develop.

The ease with which loads could be transported by water soon became recognised, and where there wasn't a suitable river, why not make an artificial version? Thus came the canal. The expediency of such transport eventually caught the imagination of a speculative public, and soon grandiose schemes were under way to promote the various canal companies hoping to cash in on the latest transport craze. Craze it often was in the scramble to get in on the latest money-spinning venture, with spades turning soil in the most unlikely and impossible places as well as in those well planned.

Thus, some schemes fell flat on their faces whilst others prospered, and the country was opening up with the new boom in transport. Still in the background laboured the horse and cart, and it had long been recognised that the firmer and flatter the surface on which the horse and cart worked, the easier it was to move heavy loads. Such loads were themselves getting heavier as technology was now including expansion of engineering developments, from Newcomen's atmospheric pumping engines to the Bolton & Watt steam versions, the latter now powering not only pumps, but ore stamps and machinery. 'Steam' was now springing up all over the country where coal and iron could be found, and Industry was coming alive.

A cart on a double line of boards was much easier to move than on a rutted dirt track, so years before 'steam' arrived permanent lines of boards appeared in mining and quarrying complexes, simplifying transport and movement. The tramroad and plateway had arrived, greatly assisting movement of heavy loads, later to have wood strips, topped with iron strips and later still replaced with cast-iron plates and rails.

These plates and rails were to take various forms and gauges as individual areas developed.

It was inevitable that such tracks would eventually lead to canals, and even be included in the building of the canal, especially in cases where, because of terrain, the canal could not be economically continued to reach a desired spot, thus was established a transport sequence. And still the horse plodded on its weary way, as it had done almost from the time it was domesticated.

All this was to dramatically change four years into the nineteenth century. The harnessing of steam power to run on the tramroads and plateways to replace the horse caused a sensation, with great fears that (a) all horse trading would collapse or, from those entrepreneurs investing in 'steam' and its development that (b) the steam power would not catch on. Steam power developed, tramroads and plateways developed and soon the speculators were back, as they had been to form the canal boom years, this time promoting the developments of the tramroads and plateways not only in a local industrial complex to join with a canal, but to really expand to join towns and villages across the country. With the coming of steam locomotives a new horizon opened up.

As with the canal boom, all sorts of schemes and companies were floated, some a shambles, some well founded. Fortunes were made and lost, as well as reputations in this new branch of engineering. In these speculative years canal vied with canal for profits, with arguments over any junction between canals concerned with how the joint was made and who was using whose water without permission. The flattest terrain had already been earmarked and used by the canal companies, so that the 'Railways', as they now became, had to find different and often very controversial alternative routes. Permissions gained, permission refused, landowners either fully supportive or the bitterest of opponents, court cases won and lost. Railways arguing with canal companies, railways arguing between themselves, railways trying to take over their rival in an area be it another railway or the existing canal. Canals trying to turn themselves into railways (as they could, if only rarely, see the potential in so doing). The legal profession were having a field day, and couldn't lose!

Into this field there stepped a (at the time) very small predator, and things were about to change!

The Great Western Railway had arrived!

In the twenty or so years following the 1804 introduction of 'mobile steam' by Richard Trevithick, and rejected by Parliament three times from 1818, the Bill for the Stockton & Darlington Railway was passed in 1821, and the line opened September 1825. Locomotive No. 1, driven by George Stephenson himself, pulled 90 tonnes, six wagons loaded with coal and flour, a covered coach with proprietors and directors, twenty-one coal wagons fitted for passengers (reputedly loaded with 450 of them), and followed by six more coal wagons.

The potential of the Steam Railway was established at 15 miles per hour. The Great Western Railway was not far behind!

This book is the story of a small predator with a voracious appetite and even bigger ideas!

THE COACH ROAD TO BATH

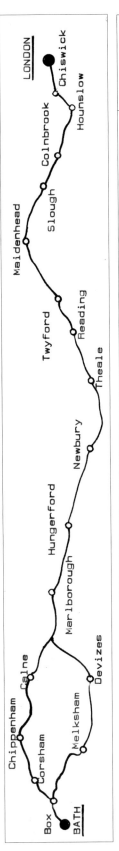

London (Hyde Park Corner)	Start	Fyfield	77
Kensington – St Mary Abbots	1¾	Overton	78
– Addison Road	2½	West Kennet	79½
Hammersmith	3¼	Beckhampton Inn	81
Turnham Green	5	Cherhill	84
Brentford – Star Gates	6	Quemerford	86¼
– Town Hall	7	Calne	87¼
Isleworth	8½	Black Dog Hill	88¾
Hounslow – Trinity Church	9¾	Derryhill	90¾
Cranford Bridge	12¼	Chippenham	93¼
Harlington Corner	13	Cross Keys	96½
Longford	15¼	Pickwick – Hare & Hounds Inn	97¼
Colnbrook	17	Box	100¼
Langley Broom – King William IV Inn	18½	Batheaston	103½
Slough – Crown Hotel	20½	Walcot	104½
Salt Hill	21¼	Bath – General Post Office	105¾
Maidenhead	26		
Littlewick	29¼		
Knowl Hill	31		
Hare Hatch	32¼		
Twyford	34		
Reading	39		
Calcot Green	41½		
Theale	44		
Woolhampton	49¼		
Thatcham	52¾		
Speenhamland	55¾		
Newbury	55¾		
Church Speen	56¾		
Hungerford	64½		
Froxfield	67		
Marlborough	74½		

List of Illustrations

Acknowledgements

Thanks are due to everyone who assisted in tracking down sources of information, from the Chief Librarian at Swindon Library to the railway employee who salvaged some records from a 'clear out' bonfire on the closure of Swindon Works. To my wife Monica, who continues to put up with someone 'with his head always stuck in a book'.

Author's Note

The many canals, plateways, tramroads and indeed other railways which had a marked influence on the development and growth of the Great Western Railway are brought together as an integrated whole in this Book.

The Sections thus form a basis from which the reader may gain an idea of the whole, or may follow and develop a specific interest. This opens up routes for further study or for just browsing the formative years of the 'Great Western' as we fondly remember it.

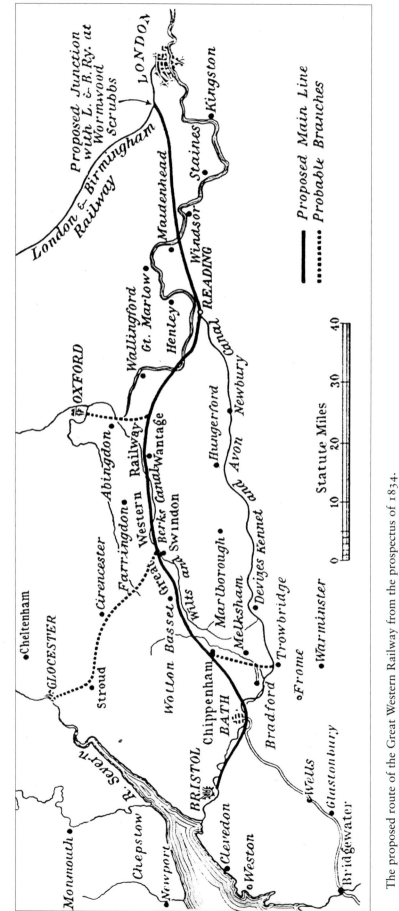

The proposed route of the Great Western Railway from the prospectus of 1834.

I

Canals

The facility of transport and communication by water has been known for centuries. There are instances of the application of a manmade canal recorded in Ancient Egypt, Greece, China, India, Russia and Europe. An early example in Britain, long before the beginnings of the 'canal boom', is that of the 'Caerdike', initiated by our Roman occupiers and cut for ease of communications between the Rivers Witham and Nene. This 40-mile cut was nominally between Peterborough and the Witham, joining about 3 miles from Lincoln. So with many innovations it was a tried and tested system which took a long time for its potential to be recognised, and for the appropriate technology to develop.

The canal systems at the time of the development of the Railway 'Boom' of the 1830–50 period were quite extensive and linked the major points of the developing industries in a quite positive if winding way. This linking was also the reason for the introduction of the railways, so immediately there was a clash of ideals and interests. There were also unlinked systems which covered specific areas and these too, being 'centres' themselves, became involved as the railway networks developed.

The basic idea of the Great Western Railway to join London to the West was already duplicated by not only the 'Great West Road' but by the existing canal system. True it was a rather winding link, embracing the use of the navigable River Avon, the Kennet & Avon Canal, then the Kennet Navigation, being the navigable stretch of the River Kennet, joining the Thames Navigation at Reading, and then winding its way via the Thames to London in one long, connected and twisting route. A northern loop, the Wilts & Berks Canal, embraced Swindon before also joining the Thames Navigation at Abingdon.

The indirectness of many canals was due to the terrain of the areas, the worry of extended costs if elaborate works were required to make a more direct route from A to B and difficulties with landowners when seeking a suitable route. The first of the two 'systems' of canals extant at the introduction of the 'Railways' (as we now understand them) was the 'individual' canal, usually a coastal location, originating from some point inland, such as a mining or agricultural centre, and heading for a port on the coast. This may or may not incorporate part of a river, which also flowed in the direction of the sea, becoming wider, deeper and more navigable as it did so. In reality, serving little more than the immediate area, but with excellent port connections, an important, but relatively isolated area was involved for local products. For items required further afield inland, either 'import' or 'export', the pack horse trails and coach roads (where they existed), were the only additional routes available for overland transport.

There was of course the excellent connection to the biggest 'canal' of the lot, the open coastal water which gave access to other ports around Britain, and hence an extensive peripheral trade route, with extensive commercial traffic (which later included delivery of the first Great Western locomotives).

There was also great opposition from some quarters to development of canals, for the obvious reason that local road or coastal hauliers would suffer, and that centres of commerce could shift due to canal influences! The same arguments would be heard later, applied to the burgeoning railways.

The second type of canal was that which joined two inland points, again winding, but which, with other linked canals and navigable rivers incorporated, gave an internal interlinked system in much the same way as railway networks were destined to do.

This canal system was generally confined to the central areas of the country where industry and commerce had their power bases, stretching roughly to say Lancaster and York at the northern end, and London–Bristol at the opposite extremity. The whole, particularly in the South and South Wales, bounded by the 'coastal' applications mentioned previously.

A major difficulty with cross-country traversing by canal was that of either diverting around the hills, adding to mileage, or of tackling the hills themselves. This gave a choice of alternatives which included both civil and mechanical engineering projects. Cuttings could be excavated, hills could be tunnelled through, or 'locks' could form the route up one side and down the other, the negotiation of the latter, when completed, all very tedious and time-consuming. Also time-consuming was the 'Inclined Plane', a mechanical arrangement where a boat may be dragged (by various methods) physically up a slope from one canal branch to another on a different level.

A further example of the transfer of a boat to a different level is that of the 'vertical lift', a time-consuming engineering achievement with the complete vessel lifted vertically and deposited in another stretch of water. Yet another mechanical appliance was that of the 'transporter bridge', where again the complete boat and its cargo were physically moved.

What could be classed as the ultimate in canal engineering is the Barton Swing Aqueduct on the 'modern' Bridgwater Ship Canal. This huge swinging tank 235 ft long, 6 ft deep and 18 ft wide carried the first commercial canal, the Duke of Bridgwater's nearly 30 ft above and at right angles to, the later ship canal below. The water is retained in the aqueduct when it is required to open to allow passage of large vessels, and the combined weight to be swung is about 1,400 tonnes. These latter examples of mechanical assistance could only be economically applied to a very active and prosperous system, as building and subsequent maintenance costs were very high.

The railway had the advantage over these mechanical appliances in not requiring such assistance anyway, and the only 'incline' tackled would be a hill which may require a 'banker' locomotive.

To all 'rules' there are exceptions, of course, and there were occasions when, for example on the Hayle Railway, rope-hauled assistance was required to control the ascent and descent of locomotives and stock on certain slopes. These were usually sharp, special descents due to coast terrain leading to quays and wharfs. As locomotive braking improved, such assistance faded from use, but in the early days of inefficient or even non-existent brakes, this was an essential for safety. The systems were operated in the same way as the canal inclined planes, so again we have the railway/canal similarities, often with ascending 'empties' balancing loads.

An example of the problem of locks is that of the famous Devizes Flight of twenty-six on the Kennet & Avon rising up like tiers in a sports stadium. Tunnelling was a last resort when too deep for a cutting to be made, again a costly and time-consuming business, in all aspects allied to railway building. The locks are costly to maintain and time-consuming to negotiate.

The basic principles of canal building are akin to those of a railway system, although sometimes including several quite major 'engineering' requirements as mentioned above: preparation of a flat bed with as few gradients as possible, the need to form cuttings where appropriate, and embankments over shallow dips in the ground using the spoil from tunnels and cuttings.

Finally comes the use of bridging or 'aqueducts' over deeper gullies, valleys and rivers over which the canal is continued by a specially designed water carrying stone and (often) iron bridge.

In summary, the construction of canals was in a number of aspects far more difficult than the building of a railway system, many problems of geology and engineering appearing for the first time, and of course having to be solved for the first time.

There was another problem which had to be solved on the introduction of a canal. What type of boat was suitable for the transport of the very varied cargoes which the vessels would carry? There was a great range of requirements. River traffic could use sailing vessels which could carry around 80 tonnes, were 100 ft long and around 18 ft wide with 70-ft masts. At the other end of the scale there were 'Tub Boats' for use on waterways known as 'tub boat' canals, the little vessels carrying only a few tonnes. In all cases it was obviously essential that the vessel had to be made with a width suitable for the differences of lock on a particular canal series.

There were various adaptations to selected boats, some with wheels built in on the bottom so that they could be used on the inclined planes of specific canals. The famous Coalbrookdale Ironmaster, John Wilkinson, built and launched the first iron barge on the River Severn in 1787, but it was to be many years before the iron-built vessel was really accepted and ousted the traditional wood construction.

Surprisingly, power beside the traditional horse was used; steam was tried later on numerous occasions but did not completely serve the purpose, and at the other end of the scale, manpower was used. Men were employed to pull the barges along, gangs of men pulling on ropes. Thomas Telford, writing in the 1790s, referred to the practice as a 'barbarous and expensive custom'. As an example, about 150 men were employed, trudging and pulling the 24 miles between Bewdley and Coalbrookdale. Telford commented that savings of two-thirds could be made by employing horses, but the manual pulling still persisted in several areas, until the demise of the canal.

Another man-powered chore, which we would today look on aghast, was that of 'legging'. Recorded on occasions as 'notoriously bad characters', the 'leggers' waited at either end of a canal tunnel, to be employed to 'leg' the barge through. This entailed laying on a board attached to the barge and 'walking' along the wall or roof of the tunnel, spiked hobnailed boots gripping the brickwork and thus propelling the barge along, really an awful form of work, but in reality it could be said that the men were at least employed and earning toward supporting their families, but it was certainly a hard existence. Some barges were poled through the tunnels.

The horse was the main power source, and where appropriate was also used on river navigations, the barges equally as big as the sailing versions but without the sails. The tow paths often stopped short of a tunnel or bridge, and this meant unshackling the horse and leading it, by means of a special path around a tunnel, or across the road over the bridge to be re-harnessed the other side. Horses were sometimes owned by the carrier, or hired from the canal authorities, and treatment of the animals ranged from very good to appalling! It took a long time for a 'Cruelty to Horses' Act to come into force (1823), and the year after saw the foundation of the RSPCA, thus embracing all animals.

The early canal boom produced canals in profusion in the late 1700s. In Wales those initiated included the Glamorganshire (1790), Neath (1791), Aberdare (1793) 6 miles long from a junction with the Glamorganshire Canal, Monmouthshire (1792), Brecknock and Abergavenny (1793), and the Swansea (1794) acquired by Great Western Railway 1872 closed 1921. With the exception of the first, all were absorbed eventually by the Great Western Railway. Another later company founded the Kidwelly & Llanelly Canal and Tramroad Company in 1812, (in 1865 converting to a railway system over its own bed). Most of these canals were interlinked to quite extensive tramway systems, of which more later.

As mentioned in the Introduction, some schemes fell by the wayside. Examples of these early casualties of 1793 canal mania include a lack of funding which killed off the Brecon to Hay and Whitney venture, difficult landowners scotched the Abergavenny to Hereford proposal, and 'excessive costs' put paid to the linking canal joining the Leominster to the Montgomeryshire. It should be noted that almost a quarter of a century later the proposed routes of the two former were covered by tramroads, following the early advice of Thomas Telford!

The 'boom' of 1790 was not to last and, following the first boom which had frizzled out by 1778, itself ended four years later. By this time fifty-five new canals had been established. Share floating and the allied subscription lists, opened in several places where speculators had decided were good 'centres' for clientele, were subjected to masses of travellers anxious to get their names on the lists before they closed as fully subscribed, and much hustling, pushing and even fighting resulted in the rush to pick up the pen and sign in.

This rush had been greatly influenced by the successes of speculators with the first boom whose investments had greatly increased in value. Even when established, takeover and competition were always there to effect returns on capital; returns which were to diminish as the railways established.

As with the absorption of railways by other railways, so with the canals, an example being the purchase of the Brecknock & Abergavenny by the Monmouthshire in 1865. The Monmouthshire could also see which way the winds of development were blowing, and turned itself into the Monmouthshire Railway & Canal Company, joining the Great Western Railway in 1875.

The 'tramway' or plate railways, often with individual gauges to suit the whim of the builder, and with track beds inadequate to the increasing weight when steam arrived, were further developed into railways proper. The use of the canals continued alongside these rapidly developing railways to assist with the movement of increasing tonnages of ore, coal, tinplate, iron etc. from the area, itself caught in an increased productivity boom. Once the railways had become established, the canals received less and less attention and hence revenue from transportation fees.

The plate and tram railways continued in joint use for many years; in total, from inception, possibly half a century, but their inadequacies became rapidly obvious. Some standardisation was required for steam introduction.

The use of horses on the tramways caused confusion and delays when a slow-moving horse-drawn train of maybe two wagons used a steam train track. With steam locomotives breaking the plates and rails, and horses delaying progress, 'standard' gauge railways were really the only answer. In the early years, very narrow tracks were established, and whilst later on, in Wales particularly, the 4-ft 8½-in gauge in general use was preferred and really the only possible answer to development, and related to hilly terrain and very tight curves. The Great Western Railway 7-ft 0¼-in broad gauge was not a practical proposition in these circumstances, and was of necessity elbowed out. Some tramways, within a mining complex and over difficult terrain, often retained their much narrower gauge tram track until the end of viability of the complex itself.

On the subject of 'gauge', and having earlier said that the basic principles of canal building are akin to those of railway construction, there were three problems which assisted in the downfall of the canal systems. One of these was the fragmented approach and reaction by the individual canal companies not only to the developing railways, but also to each other, caused in no small measure by their own organisation. No seemingly joint effort was made either to oppose the railways or to co-operate with each other for the benefit of all. Each seemed to be wrapped up in itself hoping the problems would go away, which of course they never would. The second is a familiar problem, the differences of 'gauge', a strange sounding problem when applied to canals, but familiar enough in the railway world.

Many canals were not only of different depth and width to that of their neighbours but often had sections of different width and depth in their own length, with different sizes of lock to suit the differing sections, thus severely restricting the size of boats used.

The fragmentation of the system meant that to journey from say Birmingham to London required travel over six different waterways, whilst to Hull involved no less than nine, in the latter case the railway problem of 'gauge change' was apparent and cargoes had to be transhipped. An integral problem also was that of the multiplicity of general carriers independently using in effect someone else's canal! These were thus 'carriers' and not canal owners.

It must be acknowledged, however, that the financing of canals was somewhat different from that of the railways. The canal was regarded, like a road, as a 'common highway', and in this respect the builders or companies owning the canal could not, in almost every instance, operate their own barges, such operation forbidden under their 'Acts' allowing canal construction. This situation existed throughout the complete 'boom' life of the canal system, to around 1845 when the railway had shown its commercial opposition and it was really too late anyway. Although able to trade on their own canals, the ownership of barge fleets by the canal owners could have altered the whole pattern of canal prosperity.

Canals could thus only be used by many small transport companies who were prepared to pay the tolls and abide by the canal bye-laws, but such a situation gave a very fragmented base on which to operate a commercial undertaking of such potential, at least before the railways came. Considering the expenses involved in making a canal, the only returns available to the canal company were thus the tolls which the carriers paid, based on a per ton-mile basis, lessening as mileage increased. It was, incidentally, not until 1922 that the railways adopted the per ton-mile measurement for accounting purposes.

It is thought-provoking to speculate what would have occurred if the burgeoning railway companies had been forced by their 'Acts' to follow the canal pattern; 'carriers' paying tolls to use the tracks, maintained and developed by the railway companies! It is even more thought-provoking to come forward to modern times and consider the same arrangements! Do we get a better service from toll-paying private companies running trains on separately owned track? The idea of those controlling our transport destiny was implemented in 1996 with the fragmentation of the railway system. To date (2010) it appears to have introduced a deteriorating whole! Criticism has been rapid and intense, and relating to everything from track condition to time keeping. Things can only improve.

It is of interest to note that much written about the 27-mile Stockton & Darlington line, renowned for Stephenson's 'Locomotion' but also using horses and stationary engines, first operated on a toll basis, 97 per cent of receipts being for transportation of coal, passengers an insignificant return, the payments following the established turnpike and canal system.

In modern times the Pullman Company was involved in a similar pattern of events. Could it (should it?) happen again using a similar premise? It could, and it has, also running into severe criticism concerning condition of rolling stock and attitudes of staff. As above mentioned, things can only improve. Can they?

However to return to the context of this chapter, and the haphazard controlling facets of canal management.

A railway company could nip in and take over one of the key canals in a system, and then proceed to strangle the rest by forcing traffic onto the railway by controlling the freight rates. Within forty years of its inception, the Great Western had expended almost £1 million for a return financially of a miniscule £300 in obtaining control of certain canals which it had no intention of running as going concerns!

Yet another reason for canal downfall was the speed potential of the railway, as loco design progressed, which left canal traffic literally standing.

There are a number of instances of canals, seeing the growth of railway opposition, which had the thought of converting by using their tunnels and cuttings and bed as the basis for a tracked railway! Such enterprises certainly put them in even stronger opposition with any proposed railway which often had to follow roughly the course of the canal as being the flattest route, to which they, the railways, had been beaten.

Both railway and canal promoters were well aware of this possibility. A Canal Board very quick off the mark, when the potential of railways had become obvious to some, caused a proposal to be put forward as early as 1836 for the Thames & Severn Canal Company to change itself into a railway. The Cheltenham & Great Western Union Railway, connecting Stroud, Gloucester and Cheltenham, would run virtually parallel to the canal from Cirencester to Stroud, and would start at Swindon. The Thames & Severn appreciated their potential and their position!

The canal already followed the best track location, and had the advantage of an existing tunnel at Sapperton. Not only did the canal company oppose the Bill for the Cheltenham & Gloucester Great Western Union Railway (C&GWU), but jumped in with their own Bill to change themselves, like Cinderella's pumpkin, into a railway.

At this time there were several Bills milling about, all with Cheltenham in mind. There was the broad gauge Cheltenham & Great Western Union Railway proposal and the 4-ft 8½-in gauge long-winded title of the Cheltenham, Oxford & London & Birmingham Union Railway (CO&L&BUR) connecting the London & Birmingham Railway and Tring, via Aylesbury, Oxford, Burford and Northleach, to Cheltenham.

To complicate matters, the canal company supported the CO&L&BUR as being far enough away not to affect trade whilst opposing the line including Swindon. In the event, the line starting at Swindon won the day, and by the time it was completed in 1845, the founding company, the Cheltenham & Great Western Union Railway, had been absorbed by the Great Western; the first of many.

In the 1860s there were further proposals for 4-ft 8½-in gauge tracks to compete with the broad gauge in the area of the Severn, as the Great Western Railway had all but obliterated the profitability of the Thames and Severn Canal. Maintaining part canal and part railway, the proposing Bills foundered on a technical problem dealing with transfer of water to maintain the canal portion involved in the proposal. The Severn & Thames Railway scheme collapsed.

The canal struggled on into the 1870s, and the Great Western was always very much aware of the fact that a potential railway still lurked along the reeds of its bed.

There were several reasons why railways purchased canals. One was of course that in the early years they formed competitors for the transporting of the goods of the area. Another was that often Bills for railways could not be approved in Parliament unless there was co-operation and agreement between railway and canal companies. A third was that the proposed railway had its eye on the actual course of the canal, with its existing cuts and tunnels, to form the course of the railway itself.

There was yet another way in which railways could gain control of a canal without the need for Parliament to know anything about it officially. Searching for legal ways to take over those waterways which would be of use to them, or which could cause them problems, in whatever way they had in mind, someone dug into the 'Canal Carriers' Act' of 1845. In the small print was found the clause that if a railway owned a canal it was allowed to lease others! Railways could thus band together, lease a canal which they considered in opposition, and then proceed to strangle it!

It was also found that if a group of private individuals decided to purchase a canal, they could lease it to whosoever they chose. Thus several cases arose of canal purchases being leased back immediately to the competing railway company, in one instance the purchasing group being officers of the railway company itself! Business practices change very little! Astute or sharp whichever way you choose to look at it, with the canal at the receiving end.

As a general observation concerning canals and railways, and the acquisition of the former by the latter over the years, well over three-quarters of all canals owned by railways were acquired during the late 1840s. There was at least one case of the reverse procedure, a railway leased to a canal (the Lancaster), but this was outside the Great Western Railway's sphere, and in any case the agreement was soon reversed.

A fifth reason for canal ownership by a railway, rather an artful move, was based really on the third reason noted above. It was due to the controversy over many years between canals and railways, the former fighting a losing battle all the way, that the 'Regulation of Railways Act' of 1873 came into force. Commissioners had to approve the overall control of a canal by a railway company; both railways and canals controlled by railways had to publish their rates for transport of goods to eliminate 'hidden' competition, and railways had to 'maintain the canals they already controlled'. It was this latter that was the sting in the tail.

If a railway already had a route from A to B, and a canal, basically on the same route, proposed using itself, converted, into an opposing railway route, then the railway made every effort to purchase the canal to actually keep it as a canal! It could then do a minimum of maintenance as required by the Act, and by slow neglect allow the canal to die; then it could obtain a closure, and later an abandonment order. Such was the fate of the Thames & Severn. Its last dividend was paid in 1864; it struggled on, an ex-Great Western Railway Director and Chairman becoming involved in the 1870s, possibly with the complete closure of the canal and with railway potential in mind. With the closure proposition heavily opposed by other businessmen and canal owners, the proposal again collapsed and the Great Western Railway bought out his interest, profitably for him.

The canal deteriorated further through lack of attention, and protests from others associated with the waterway triggered from the Great Western Railway a closure notice on 26 miles of canal. Various Local Authority bodies became involved in opposition, and in 1895 a trust was set up for the canal, giving the local bodies powers to operate as a canal but not allowing them to resurrect the thought of turning it into a railway. Considerable sums were spent, and the canal reopened in 1904, but it was much too late. With the railway potential threat removed, the Great Western Railway lost interest and the canal finally closed in the late 1920s.

The Wilts & Berks Canal was a different matter and was a simple case as far as the Great Western Railway was concerned. Its route and purpose were so like those of the Railway Company that it was completely ruined by the railway. Its receipts massively slashed, by the 1870s alone from £15,000 per year to just over £1,000, and in desperate attempts to improve its fortunes, management resigned and the canal itself changed hands several times. The Great Western considered purchase, whether to assist or to add confusion to the problems of the canal, then eventually dropped out of the market. Receipts fell even further. An opposed closure in 1897 caused it to flounder on, but with a complete cessation of traffic by 1906, it had closed and been abandoned by 1914. Remains of the canal, and of its feeder (the North Wiltshire Canal) to the Thames & Severn, both visible to Brunel and Gooch on their visit to select a factory site, can still be seen in Swindon. The latter's course, now a pedestrian and cycle track, still runs under the centre of the site of the railway works, itself now mostly abandoned as its early competitors had been years ago. Fate has turned the wheel full circle. The works site is now a large shopping complex and some of the original buildings now house 'STEAM', the museum of the Great Western Railway.

It is rather ironic that in the early years of construction of Swindon Works, the network of local canals transported, in effect, some of the means of their own destruction. The transport in quantity of coal, coke, iron and other materials was easier, if slower, by canal in the quantities required before the railway actually went anywhere in a completed and organised way. Once organised, the railway took over, virtually completely, not only its own requirements but that of 'local' traffic as well.

It is difficult to imagine this land of ours without railways, so accustomed to them have we now become. Without railways, and with very mediocre roads, how indeed were the first locomotives delivered to the Great Western Railway from the manufacturers. The only method was by water – coastal and river included. The first locomotive delivered to Gooch for the Great Western Railway travelled by sea from Liverpool finishing the journey by water, being then manhandled onto a short length of hastily laid track, which initially did not go anywhere. The same fate befell 'North Star' which was delivered to Maidenhead and there had to slumber in a field until the tracks arrived several months later.

The original 'London to Bristol' railway, the early name of the Great Western, was proposed to run on a more direct southerly route than that which included Swindon, and basically followed the route of a direct canal system. The intense opposition to the proposal led to it being routed in a northerly curve which at the time passed through empty countryside, the only large cities being at the extremities of the tracks.

To the south of Swindon the direct Bristol–London canal link was full of trepidation in the early days of railway competition. A proposal for the 'London, Newbury & Bath Railway' submitted on behalf of the Kennet & Avon Canal, as early as 1845, to turn itself into a railway was not successful. It was probably a move to push the opposing railway into making some sort of offer or proposal, and in this it succeeded, as the Great Western Railway and the Wiltshire, Somerset & Weymouth Railway Company came to an agreement over the future of the canal and its assets. The pressure continued, and in 1852 the Great Western Railway agreed to take over the canal with the result previously mentioned! The Kennet & Avon Canal was still a problem to Brunel, who had to have a section diverted to clear his railway route.

Canal and rail rivalries abounded in other areas of what would become eventually all within, or most within the mantle of the Great Western. An interesting and existing remnant of the canal and river traffic in the South West is that of the Morwellham Quay and associated works on the Tamar. This whole complex of mines, canal, inclined plane and river quay is well restored and forms a worthwhile visit to a pre-railway site. The rights included in the land agreements gave mining and mineral finds a prominent position and rich veins of copper were struck when the canal tunnel was driven. Throughout the century the area mines prospered or otherwise according to the market forces, but the overall prosperity anticipated was never fully realised, the boom of the war years of around 1800 died with the peace that followed.

The 1850s saw railway competition becoming a real worry to the proprietors, the South Devon & Tavistock Railway opposition was too strong, and the profitability of the associated Tavistock Canal, doubtful from the start, dropped away as receipts fell. By the 1880s, it was no longer viable, and before the century's turn had ceased operating.

Whilst many canals fudged and struggled with the railway threat, or closed eyes and ears in isolation whilst others around them lost out in the struggle, the Torrington Canal owner said at a meeting that he would, in effect 'be glad to see the canal superseded by a more useful and convenient mode of transit and communication'. With an aqueduct becoming part of a road, and the one inclined plane cut in half by the rail tracks, that was that, and by 1870 the canal ceased to exist; certainly an example of 'if you can't beat 'em, join 'em!' and a realistic approach to a real problem.

Probably the strangest thing of all about the situation was that the canal company pressed for a railway! And whilst the London South Western obtained an Act for such a venture, the estimated receipts and cost put them off somewhat and they then attempted to abandon the project. In this they were firmly opposed by the canal owner who insisted that such a railway should go ahead! A complete reversal of the usual approach to railway/canal matters of the period.

After virtually fifty years of proposals and counter-proposals regarding various costs applied to various routes, the 'Bude Harbour and Canal' system opened in 1823. With a length of railway and six inclined planes incorporated, the actually completed length of 36 miles of canal carried 'manure' in small tub boats inland to the agricultural areas surrounding the waterway. The 'manure' was not what we would now suppose, but was sand from the beach, used in place of lime and formed from shells, crushed by countless tides.

For transport of goods in the opposite direction a short length of the canal from Bude Harbour could take ships up to 300 tonnes, and larger barges were proposed, capable of handling 50 tonnes of sand at a time. The smaller tub boats were hauled up one inclined plane by ropes and chains attached to massive buckets filled with water which descended down into deep wells. There, a mechanism allowed the water to drain out of the bucket, thus allowing the counter weighted machinery to reverse. A balance was obtained with boats going down the planes. Large water wheels up to 50-ft diameter operated winding drums on other planes, and one had a standby steam engine, if problems arose with the 'free' power of the waterwheel. Waterwheels also operated the maintenance workshop machinery, which included a metal turning lathe.

Financial problems increased, and mechanical failures followed suit, one conditioning the other. Over a period of fifty years, no dividends had been paid to shareholders, and then a very brief period followed when debts had been paid off, for a very small return to be made, decreasing all the time for about eight years. The effects of the broad gauge Launceton & South Devon Railway as the transportation of the area caused the seeking of support from those with business interests in the Bude Canal to add 'and Launceston Junction Railway Co.' to its name, and form such a company to join the canal and the railway. The move was not successful, and canal receipts continued downward.

By 1877, one of the main traders using the canal had ceased operating, and the canal bought the related vessels and wagons. Rising freight rates on the canal by the new company nominally leasing the vessels to start afresh caused the decline in receipts to accelerate. Artificial fertilisers had almost destroyed the sand trade, by appearing, in bulk, by rail. By the 1890s, parts of the system were closing down, and moves to utilise the water of the canal and reservoir also staggered to a halt. The canal as such closed and was abandoned as a waterway by Act of 1912.

During the 1700s, several small canals were extant in the South West, with the purpose of conveying sand and lime to various farmlands in the area, and, in the opposite directions, transport of the produce of various mines to the coast. A very early example of the latter was that of Parnall's Canal, dug from the Carelaze mine around 1720. The canal had direct access to the mine by tunnel, which apparently collapsed a dozen years later and trapped the little boats inside. The boats were rediscovered during survey work in the 1850s. There are about 42 miles of tunnel or 'underground' canal within the country's canal complex, including other rivers with direct canal access.

A canal which had an alternative in its Act was that of the Liskeard & Looe Union, when its initiating meeting of 1823 approved building 'a canal or railroad'. Canals were known, but railroads as such were unknown quantities, so the canal option was favoured. A very mixed traffic was envisaged, with coal in and agricultural produce out as the two mainstays, and whilst tolls were set for other items, copper ore in the quantities eventually transported from the Caradon mines was not envisaged at the time. The railway opposition, which soon became very obvious, was opposed vigorously when proposed in the 1840s, but the company was supportive of the Liskeard & Caradon Railway, with which was associated certain members of the Board of the canal! The Liskeard & Caradon Railway was of the horse-drawn variety, but it was the major steam versions to which exception was being taken, and it was a branch of the Steam Cornwall Railway that caused some misgivings when proposed to include Looe. A special clause was forced into the Act of the Railway Company to ensure the rivals would talk about the problems envisaged, more of a fudge than a practical solution!

Such was the output drive of the mines, however, that the canal could not cope, and even proposed building their own railway to Looe, emphasising that the lines would augment the canal and not close it down! Costs were to be relatively cheap as the canal company already owned most of the land, and the railway would follow the course of the canal. The new Liskeard & Looe Railway had greater capacity than the canal! Within about a decade, however, the boom years of the mines were over, and the Liskeard & Caradon Railway bankrupt. Its debts to the Liskeard & Looe Canal & Railway Company were such that even this company was in difficulties, and to complicate matters, the former Liskeard & Cardon Railway was leased to the latter, which was itself joined into the Great Western system in 1901. Worked by the Great Western Railway it was absorbed completely into the Great Western as one of the 'benefits' of the 1923 amalgamations. Whatever plans existed to continue working the canal, the Great Western approach to canals was well known, and appears to have been applied in this case, the canal very quickly ceasing to function.

A later Great Western Railway constituent railway, the Bristol & Exeter, had come under a competition situation with the Grand Western Canal. This canal was to be yet another proposed link between the Bristol and English Channel, a total of about 46 miles. It was not to be and only a portion was completed, complicated by the inclusion of seven lifts and an inclined plane with a rise of 81 ft. The lifts were brick chambers which held a pair of side-by-side iron tanks, counterbalanced by each other and supported on chains. A small tub boat or barge could be run into a tank, the ends shuttered off, and either water and/or another barge in the other tank provided the counterbalance weight for movement to the new level of canal required; practical but costly engineering requirements, although reputedly quicker ton for ton than an equivalent lock arrangement.

The Bristol & Exeter had opened in 1844 and its branch to Tiverton in 1848 had really chopped the canal traffic. Rates for goods were driven lower and lower, the railway being able to do this, financed by its other interests, but the canal could not compete. The only people to benefit were the local population with almost free transport, but the situation could not continue, and when the railway involved the Bridgwater & Taunton Canal, threatening the Grand Western even further, something in the struggle had to give way.

Within ten years traffic disappeared and the railway finalised the purchase of the Grand Western. Various portions were eventually closed, abandoning the lifts and inclined plane sections allowed a very small section toward Tiverton to remain for stone traffic which eventually ceased in the 1920s. It was however, to be another forty years before the British Transport Commission, as it had evolved, eventually abandoned the remnant of the Grand Western Canal.

The Bristol & Exeter Railway, after its epic struggle with price cutting and machinations with the Bridgwater & Taunton Canal, was, on its victory, almost immediately itself absorbed in 1876 into the Great Western Railway, waiting in the wings for someone else to sort out the problem.

The Bridgwater & Taunton Canal itself had had a struggle for existence from its opening, rather late in the canal saga in 1827. The Tone River (which had been made navigable in part in 1638 and completely navigable by about 1760), had as its guardians the 'Conservators', and this body had opposed by all means possible (including stopping the water supply) the establishment of the Bridgwater & Taunton Canal. This animosity overflowed in a forcible seizure of the Tone by the canal company when its (the Tone Company's) outstanding debts to the canal company could not be paid. Eventually forced to court and then officially taking over the Tone group for a payment of £10,000, the canal found a clause inserted in the ruling to keep the river navigable, the latter neglected during the dispute.

Water was obviously a major factor in all canals and was very jealously guarded by the individual canal companies. If two canals, because of an agreement, were to be connected for mutual benefit, there was usually a clause somewhere in the agreement that no 'water' was to be lost to either canal in the subsequent use of the junction. A special form of lock, known as a 'stop lock', was installed at such places to ensure no loss or transfer of water from one system to the other occurred when vessels moved from canal to canal.

The disputes among the various fragmented canal bodies themselves made them possibly easier prey to the burgeoning railway system in early railway years. A canal to actually benefit from the railway was the Exeter, as it connected to a port and thus had an advantage to start with. Part opened as early as 1566, it was to some extent affected by both the South Devon branch for both broad and standard gauge, and the Bristol & Exeter. In an early attempt to further increase its capacity, towing by steamers was introduced, but because of damage to the canal banks was not continued, and horse traction only was retained for a long period.

In the 1840s, a grandiose scheme was proposed to link the Bristol and English Channels, and involved several railway and canal companies, and several canal companies which fancied adding 'Railway' to their titles. When in 1848 the Bristol & Exeter Railway opened its Tiverton branch, it was not connected directly to Bridgwater, so the local Corporation built the 'Communication Works', which was a horse tramway joining up wharves on the River Parrett to the railway (later steam traction). In the boom years there were thoughts of a Bridgwater & Taunton Canal and Railway, as well as a Chard Canal Company and Chard Railway Company, with a 'Bristol and English Channels Connection Railway and Harbours Company'!

This proliferation of railways also encompassed the Kennet & Avon Canal in a bid to promote a London, Newbury & Bath Direct Railway, joined to the London, Devizes and Bridgewater direct. The whole system was to be known as the 'West of England Central and Channels Junction Railway', with a further proposal to link into the proposed Devon & Cornwall Central Railway. The Great Western Railway and the Bristol & Exeter Railway would now have to face up to a series of alternative routes through their preserves! And even the Tone Conservators threatened to jump onto the bandwagon if the proposed lines in any way jeopardised the future of the canal, at which point they would reopen the river to navigation. The Bridgwater & Taunton Canal would have added 'and Stafford Railway and Harbour Company' to their title had the scheme actually unfolded, but it faded away, money, expertise and the necessary conviction found wanting.

It must be said that the Bridgwater & Taunton Canal was quite well maintained by the Bristol & Exeter Railway, which purchased it and the Grand Western and the Chard Canals in 1864, 1866 and 1867, before being absorbed by the Great Western Railway. Ten years later with the inevitable fate concerning the canals included with the purchase.

The joining of the English and Bristol Channels was also the idea behind the 'Public Devonshire Canal', an extension proposed by the eight miles of the (also proposed) Exeter & Crediton Navigation Company, the whole being about 48 miles in length. A start of sorts was made, but eventually was discontinued.

Another very late starter, in canal terms, had been the Chard Canal, 14 miles long and opened in 1841. Proposed with two lifts and two inclined planes, it had to rise a height of 230 ft in its length, and it ran straight into the competition of the Bristol & Exeter Railway which almost immediately started to take its traffic. The Chard was also in competition with the Westport Canal and, seeing the way in which the 'Railway' wind was blowing, obtained an act to convert to a railway in 1846. By this time, both the Bristol & Exeter Railway and London South Western Railway were fencing with each other for control and were watching each other's moves very closely. Eventually a legal compromise was reached, the London South Western Railway purchasing the railway on its opening in 1863, whilst the Bristol & Exeter bought the canals.

There were other small canals formed in the Somerset area by the extended use of land drainage channels, two examples of very small lengths less than 2 miles long were those of Galton and of Brown, which reverted back to a drainage roll after involvement in the overall canal picture of the period.

The Bristol & Exeter Railway, opened in 1842, was chasing the Glastonbury Canal, experiencing difficulties with flooding. In opposition, the Bristol & Exeter Railway formed and backed the Somerset Central Railway whose new broad gauge tracks followed the side of the canal. All within part of the 'deal', the Somerset Central was leased to the Bristol & Exeter Railway, but the canal was excluded and was later abandoned although part survived until 1936. The Somerset Central Railway later became part of the, by now, standard gauge Somerset & Dorset Railway.

In railway opposition was of course any river which could be made navigable, and an example also in great competition with and opposed by the Chard Canal Company had been the proposed Parrett Navigation Co. which opted for commercial success using the Parrett as a readymade canal! In 1845 the whiff of railway steam was experienced and the proposed Bath & Exeter Junction Railway had also put in a bid for the Somerset Coal Canal. Within a decade, canal receipts had halved due to railway opposition, and the enterprise was taken over by the 'Land Drainage Commissioners' as trade had almost gone by the 1870s, the company dying in 1878.

A move to involve again Bristol and the English Channel stemmed from a 1792 idea to link Bristol to Poole by means of a canal, using also part of the Avon at Bath with connections to Mendip Collieries. With great enthusiasm the project started, with again proposals for a lift for boats up to 10 tonnes. The lift was built and successfully used for a trial run but the cash ran out before the enthusiasm, and the project, as so many before, and after, died long before completion.

The list of constituent and associated companies included in the next chapter mentions various 'tramways', which were almost inevitably linked with canals, forming the continuation where it was undesirable or impractical to run a waterway. Among the rivers and canals associated with such tramways may be mentioned the River Tiegn, and the Hackney and Stover Canals. The linking Stover Canal of 1792 carried china clay for the potteries, and stone was transported by the Haytor Granite Tramroad, its 'rails' being granite slabs with a 4-ft 3-in 'track' groove. The tramroad 'joined' the Moreton Hampstead and South Devon Railway (originally the Newton and Moreton Hampstead Railway). The Hackney Canal was leased from the South Devon Railway in 1862 and later from the Great Western by various operators, but by 1928 the Hackney ceased operating, followed by the Stover a few years into the 1930s. The First World War had prolonged the life of both canals to a great extent, but other transport had taken over the role of effective carriers by road, and remaining canal traffic diminished rapidly.

Another very small canal, with its own inclined plane and associated with a tramway, was the Par Canal opened in the railway era in 1847. Less than 2 miles long, it joined the mining interests of J. Treffry with the harbour at Par, but fell afoul of the route of the Cornwall Minerals Railway, driving its rails from Par to Fowey. The tramway was quickly taken over by the growing railway which found no use for the canal, and it inevitably closed in 1873. This example shows that even small railways also formed impossible opposition to small canals! The Cornwall Mineral Railway fell to the Great Western Railway in 1877.

By Acts of 1811 and 1821, a Plymouth to Princetown connection had been introduced with the Plymouth and Dartmoor Horse Tramroad linking quarries by the small Cann Quarry Canal, the tramroad near the route of the later South Devon and Tavistock Railway. In all areas, then, the 'railway' was in attendance.

Another later adjunct of the Great Western Railway, the Oxford, Worcester & Wolverhampton Railway, purchased the Stratford-upon-Avon Canal and the smaller Stourbridge extension canal in 1846, again to eliminate competition. With the Stratford

Canal, the shareholders probably benefitted more from the sale than would have been the case had they stuck to their guns and maintained a faith in the viability of the canal. The Great Western took over the Oxford, Worcester & Wolverhampton Railway in 1863 and with it the Stratford-upon-Avon Canal, which inevitably became un-navigable.

Similar sales were happening in various parts of the railway system all over the country, the strongest case for the actual retention of canals being on the northern limits of the Great Western Railway, into the industrial heartland of the Midlands where often railways could not get in to take over the waterways, as there was no available space suitable for rail tracks as well as the canals.

The very nature of the area and its veritable maze of canals, many interlinking between the local industrial centres, meant that even a small canal wielded considerable power due to its viability as a canal. Hence any railway bid to take over the canal for conversion into a railway fell on deaf ears as the canal companies were not interested. In some areas, even if a practical proposition, it would also have been a case of 'all or none', as one conversion in isolation would not have been truly practical and would have destroyed the linked system, forcing all others to follow suit. In the circumstances no one fell for the proposition to set a conversion in motion.

In this case the position of the canals was strengthened, and a number of railway 'basins' were introduced where rail and water met for the transfer of goods to the mutual benefit of both. In many cases, however, as little use of canals as possible was the object of the exercise.

Although much canal traffic continued to flourish, more use could have been made of the waterways than was actually made in the areas served by the 'basins', but the lack of use was certainly a major policy decision on the part of the railways. There was, however, recognition of the strong position held by the canals of the Birmingham area. The maze of small linked canals (see page 38 for a list of named branches), many augmented by short-run tramroads, carried an amazing amount of material for the works and furnaces of the area. For example, in the Dudley area there were about 120 furnaces turning out 90 tonnes of iron each per week, each ton required 7 tonnes of limestone, ore and coke for the melts.

The Great Western's Charles Saunders recognised the strength of the canal system, and along with the Oxford, Worcester & Wolverhampton Railway, agreed that the railway companies, were not really interested in very short haul traffic anyway. Saunders' comment on the situation agreed that the 'Railway was not adapted for large quantities of minerals to be carried from works for short distances ... obstructs the traffic on the main line'. The following sentence sums up the situation completely when he continued, 'I do believe a canal better adapted to short distances of traffic between mines and works.' Many of the producing sites were adjacent to the canals anyway so very little else could be done by the rail companies but to accept the situation.

The canal basin thus came into being, the system being fully supported by the railway companies, who, in retrospect really had no alternative but to get in as close as was possible to the canal carriers with wharf facilities owned by the railways. Given the situation, the canal systems were expanded, improved and updated, when canals in other parts of the country (say 1840s to 1860s) were being eliminated!

The meeting places of canal and railway were small wharfs/goods yards, and other sites for which the railway had maintenance responsibilities. These responsibilities included the lifting tackle and crane arrangements, and the lighting for the yard and goods shed etc. Some sites had delightful names! Those which spring to mind (I was then, *c.* 1960, responsible for the railway area planned preventive maintenance procedures being introduced) include such gems as Swan Village, Daisy Bank, Princes End, and Primrose Wharf. A check on all existing procedures showed great reluctance on the part of the maintenance staff to accompany me to certain sites. I soon found out why. The sites had long been abandoned, but were still on the long established maintenance schedule, and made convenient stopping off places for lunchtime sandwiches.

Whilst still ticking off the water valves, crane and lifting tackle and yard lighting on the maintenance sheet on their routine visits, at one site I found the goods deck collapsed, the lifting tackle rope slings rotted and falling apart along with the small hut where they were stored, and the wooden goods deck crane had rotted off at the bottom and had actually fallen over, lying among waist high grass, weed, and thistles!

I remember also seeing an accident report on severe injuries to a 'Lamp Attendant' who was changing light bulbs on the goods shed. For one bulb change he couldn't get the correct angle on the ladder he always carried, so he put the bottom end in a barge tied up against the wharf. As he bounced up the ladder the barge drifted out from the wharf, and down came the ladder, lamp attendant and bulb! Whilst the canal was still in use, the various sites railway-wise had been generally abandoned, probably to road transport.

The effect of railway competition with canals is well illustrated by the following tables relating to the Kennet & Avon Canal, bearing in mind the Great Western's involvement from 1852, but competition from a decade earlier.

Year	Tonnes Carried	Revenue £	Average Receipts Per Ton Shillings
1838	341,878	52,910	3.09
1848	360,610	32,740	1.87
1858	261,822	18,916	1.44
1868	210,567	11,124	0.88
1898	122,716	5,265	0.93

A change in data shows the following:

Year	Revenue £	Expenditure £
1900	5,322	8,081
1901	5,251	8,327
1902	5,094	8,436
1903	4,924	8,501
1904	4,539	9,205
1905	4,240	10,985
1906	4,171	9,228
1907	3,933	9,750
1908	4,032	9,913
1909	4,093	11,239

1910	4,226	11,184
1911	4,213	10,779
1912	3,983	10,888
TOTALS	58,031	126,516

Over the period a deficit of £68,485 accrued. Such losses could not continue in the maintenance of a waterway which seemingly no one wanted to use.

Other canals owned by the Great Western Railway Company showed similar deficit conditions. Thus for the years 1903–12:

	DEFICIT PER YEAR		
Canal	Minimum £	Maximum £	Average £
Bridgwater & Taunton	481	5,897	2,877
Great Western	16	189	93
Kennet & Avon Navigations	3,577	7,146	5,932
Monmouthshire & Brecon & Abergavenny	1,237	2,408	1,673
Stourbridge Extension	698 (profit)	925	17
Stratford-upon-Avon	424	1,117	804
Swansea	98	2,485	856
TOTAL LOSSES PER YEAR AVERAGE			12,252

The case of the Bridgwater & Taunton Canal with regard to railway opposition is further highlighted by the greatly shortened rail route to South Wales afforded by the Severn Tunnel. This had dramatic effects on the transportation of coal by canal as shown by the following table:

Year	Coal Tonnage
1880	17,072
1886	Tunnel opened
1890	7,140
1900	3,275
1905	320
1921	Canal virtually disused

The effect of the railway system generally on canals had been increasingly obvious for a number of years. One of the strange facets of canal ownership was that the Great Western did not possess a right to carry traffic by canal. Thus, whilst maintaining the waterway, it was up to others to use it! The situation was such that a Royal Commission was appointed in 1906 to examine and report on the canal system generally. With the complete viability of the canal system as a remit, dealing with finance, profitability, private or state ownership, commercial and communication benefits and particularly state support or subsidy, the Commission duly reported in great detail. A concluding statement from the report is here quoted:

> Any question of the application of state funds toward the cheapening of transportation should include consideration of every form of transport, with the object of assisting that form which is best suited to the proved requirements of the trading interests of the Nation. In other words, the question of transport must be treated as a whole. It is not within the sphere of practical politics to draw a dividing line between the different forms ... it is desirable to assist the means of transportation suitable for all kinds of traffic (i.e. Railways) [rather than] certain sections and traders only suitable for certain classes of traffic [which are] wholly inadequate for, and altogether unsuited to, the general requirements and conditions of the trading community in this country.

The canal system was finally, officially, under scrutiny, but the question at the centre of the argument 'The question of transport must be treated as a whole' is *still* being debated whilst this is being written, long after the demise of the steam railway system which had slowly but effectively strangled the canals.

Whilst our own canals were neglected and drying at the beginning of the twentieth century, the Americans were thinking big, and also tying canals into an integrated canal/railway system. Such was the difference in thinking, canals having been pushed into the background over the last fifty years of the nineteenth century, that the Royal Commission Report of 1909 proposed Nationalisation of the main routes of canals/rivers and enlargement to take 300-ton standard barges on the river sections and 100-ton vessels on the selected canals. Where suitable, expansion to take 750-ton or even 1,200-ton vessels was proposed, as the Manchester Ship Canal. The question was 'who pays?'

The report caused controversy. The railway companies could see a major problem immediately. Assuming a nationalised and expanded canal system failed to cover costs, government subsidies would create unfair competition with privately funded railways. If the system did indeed succeed, it could thus put the railway companies out of business.

The First World War caused delays in decision-making, the government controlling the canals until 1920, and whilst some improvements to certain canals were made, the nature of canal use was changing. The commercial transport of goods was giving way to pleasure boating, and as mentioned before, talk of an 'integrated' transport system continues, we appear to be no nearer to getting one!

So we currently see dedicated groups of volunteers digging out long neglected and abandoned lengths of canal with pleasure use in mind but secretly longing to once again be involved with a commercial enterprise for transport of goods currently filling our roads with bigger and bigger lorries. All power to their elbows, but theirs is likely to be a very difficult task. Whilst some canal lengths are still visible, maybe as mud and weed choked channels, many crucial portions are now completely built over.

As an example of this, the Wilts & Berks used to run through the centre of Swindon town. There are still two clearly defined lengths, but they are both sides of the rebuilt town shopping centre with no hope of ever being joined again, unless some very revolutionary planning decisions are taken. The only alternative would be to go around the town, again a daunting prospect.

To the east of Swindon, a double-arched railway bridge originally had one road arch and one canal arch. Whilst the tree and grass lined route of the canal may be seen along the side of the road, the arches now span one road lane out of Swindon and one toward Swindon so the canal route is again blocked. This situation must occur all over the country so the prospects for an integrated canal addition to solve our transport problems are currently not very good. However, a development on Swindon, publicised in February 2002, shows an included proposal for a length of new canal around Swindon and beside the M4 motorway with the proposed new development. This was again reconsidered during 2007/08 and a new scheme, completely different, was proposed. This entailed continuing the existing, and re-instated length of the Wilts & Berks Canal which entered the outskirts of Swindon from the West, to a dead end.

The new proposals have caused a great deal of controversy as they include ignoring the currently existing original canal length, which has long since been grassed over, and which continues from the refurbished length to include a 'dead end' length along the centre of a main road in a completely built up area only about 200 yds parallel to the grassed-over length.

Where or what the future holds remains to be seen, but as advertisements say, 'watch this space'.

This all ties in with the ongoing rebuilding projects of the major canals of the Great Western area; the Thames & Severn, Kennet & Avon, North Wilts, and the Wilts & Berks, the latter hopefully benefitting from the 2002 Swindon proposal, or the 2007/08 variation.

With the current congested state of Britain's road system and the current chaotic state of the railway systems is there somewhere in the waterway systems which existed a potential which could be exploited for the future? With road and rail systems appearing to get worse as time passes, if something isn't done, and soon, the transport systems of Britain will grind to a halt!

An aircraft can't pull a trailer, and the skies are becoming ever more choked as time passes, so the only other transport form so far not exploited is the inland waterway! Maybe, just maybe, something could be achieved. Integrated transport systems have been talked about long enough. It's time for a searching look before everything stops!

The early effectiveness of the railways tended to overshadow completely any other form of transport and the cutthroat competition certainly had a dramatic effect on the alternatives. Certainly on the Great Western system, any real opposition or the canals had been squashed really long before the turn of the nineteenth century. The only other opposition from the old days, the pack horse trains and the road coaches, was really no opposition at all and could be ignored.

The only real opposition now to a railway was another railway! The Great Western was continuing to pick them off one by one, carefully selecting a time and circumstance. The scale of such takeover is quite surprising and the companies taken over by the Great Western are listed in the third section of this book. However, before we examine these companies, we will look at another often-neglected 'railway' aspect, as a continuation of this canal chapter, not really any 'opposition' as such, but an important adjunct to railway history in the form of plateways and tramroads, the first 'railways'.

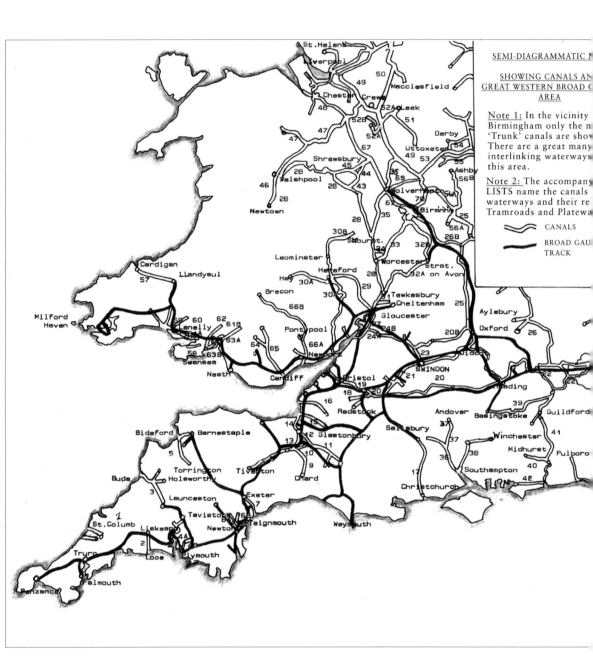

Diagrammatic map showing canals and Great Western broad gauge area. Some of the canals here are not strictly within the Great Western's sphere of influence but indicate the coastal and South West Midlands scene, as well as the Great Western Railway area.

The Main Canals of the Great Western Area

Map	Canal	Commercial Use		Length	Notes
		Opened	Closed	Miles (to nearest)	
1	St Columb	*c.* 1778	*c.* 1781	6½	
2	Liskeard & Looe Union	1828	*c.* 1861	6	Became a railway.
3	Bude	*c.* 1823	1891/1960	35	Small 'tub' boats fitted with wheels to run on inclined planes.
4a	Tavistock Canal & Tamar Navigation	*c.* 1818	*c.* 1873	6	Several inclined planes. Including waterwheel, bucket, and steam operated.
4b	Cann Quarry Canal	1829	*c.* 1835	2	
5	Torrington	1827	*c.* 1871	6	Built without an Act, thus built privately.
6a	Hackney	1843	1928	$\frac{5}{8}$	
6b	Stover	1792	1939	2	Part closed 1867.
7	Exeter (not 'nationalised' by the BTC in 1948 when most independent canals were taken over)	*c.* 1566 enlarged 1701 & *c.* 1830	Still open	5	Rebuilt 1701 & 1825–27 widened and depth increased to 15 ft. Planned to avoid river navigation.
8	Grand Western	1814	1867/1924	24½	Steam engine. Inclined plane, part closed 1867.
9	Chard	1842	*c.* 1868	13½	Taken over by the Bristol & Exeter Railway, 1860s.
10	River Tone Navigation	1717	1878/1967		Taken over by the Bridgwater & Taunton Canal.
11	Ivelchester & Langport Navigation	1795	1797	8	
12	Parrett Navigation	Part tidal navigable	1878		Associated with the Tone.
13	Bridgwater & Taunton	1827 1841 ext	*c.* 1907	15¼	In competition with the Tone river conservators with longstanding disputes. Joined by the Chard Canal.

14	River Brue Navigation	c. 1500 (part before)			Very early transport routes (also 16 below) to which joined.
15	Glastonbury	1833	c. 1854	14	Purchased by the Bristol & Exeter Railway, 1848. Became part of Somerset & Dorset Railway.
16	River Axe Navigation	c. 1500 (part before)	Part closed 1810		Associated with 14 above.
17	Hampshire Avon Navigation	1664–84	1705	36	
18	Somerset Coal Canal Note: A Dorset & Somerset Canal was not completed.	1805	1898	18	Part became tramroad 1815. Then S&DR 1871. FWR 1904. Combe Hay Tunnel (66 yds) built 1805 used for railway.
19	River Avon Navigation Upper	1639		28	Lower Avon Nav. Trust
	River Avon Navigation Lower	1639	1875	17½	OWWR then GWR 1875.
20a	Kennet & Avon Canal	1794/1810 lengths currently being opened for pleasure	1937	57	Bought by GWR 1852. To maintain water levels, two pumping stations were opened at Crofton & Claverton. Crofton is still operating with 1812 pump, now used as a 'standby'.
20b	Kennet Navigation	1723	1934	18	
21	Wilts & Berks	1810/19	1906	66	Destroyed by the Railway (partial restoration underway).
22	Thames Navigation			125	Part always navigable.

23	North Wiltshire	1819	1906	9		From the Thames & Severn running into the centre of Swindon. A branch off the Wilts & Berks. The North Wilts ran right through the centre of Swindon Railway Works.
24a	Stroud Water Canal	*c.* 1779	1941	8		A broad canal to take river traffic. Man powered early on! Had a steam dredger in 1815.
24b	Thames & Severn Canal	*c.* 1788	1911	30		Controlled by GWR. 1882–95
25	Oxford	1790	Part 1951	80		In 1790, other canals also linked the Rivers Trent, Mersey, Severn and Thames.
26a	Grand Junction	1799/1815	Part	142		Strongly objected to any canal wishing to convert to a railway!
26b	Grand Union Canal	1814	Part			Purchased by 26a 1894.
27	Gloucester & Berkeley Ship Canal (Sharpness)	1793/1827	Open	17		Expanded and prosperous.
28	Severn Navigation	1842		43		Mostly always navigable and in use.
29	Herefordshire & Gloucestershire	(Authorised 1791) 1845	1881	34		Extensive delays in completion.
30a	Wye Navigation	*c.* 1660	Part	8		
30b	Leominster Canal	1796	1858	18½		To Shrewsbury & Hereford Railway. 1858, and used as part of railway.
31	Coombe Hill Canal	1796	1876	2¾		Went into liquidation 1870s with a number of others.
32	Stratford-upon-Avon	1816	Part	26		Sold to OW&W Railway.
33	Worcester & Birmingham	1815/1836	In use	30		Bought by Sharpness Docks 1874.
34	Droitwich	1771	1916	7		Leased by Sharpness Docks. Abandoned 1939.

35	Staffordshire & Worcestershire Canal	1772/1816	Part 1949	52	Part still used. New locks 1967 with support society.
36	Salisbury & Southampton	1802	1806	13	Not finished. Insufficient funding.
37	Andover	1794	1859	22	Converted to a railway (Andover & Redbridge Railway).
38	River Ichen	1710	1869	10½	
39	Basingstoke	1794	1901	12	Classed as an agricultural canal. A financial failure due to debts. In 1866 into Liquidation but rescued several times. By 1948 semi-derelict.
40	Rivers Western Rother	1794	1888	12	An association of 40, 41 & 42 to make a through route failed although sections were opened through the 1820s. Dying in 1855 wound up completely in 1888, as a combined project.
	& Arun	1790	c. 1890	13	
41	Wey & Arun Junction Canal	1816	1871	18½	
42	Portsmouth & Arundel	1817/1831	1896/1928 (short lengths)	30	
43	Shropshire Canal & Shropshire Union Canals, the latter in 1846 combining several others.	1792	From 1801 Part to 1894	10 Union Canals over 200	Three inclined planes Union combined Ellesmere & Chester, Birmingham & Liverpool, Shrewsbury, & Montgomeryshire. Part converted to railway, leased to LNWR.
44	Donnington Wood Canal. Private canal in Shropshire (Duke of Sutherland).	1768	c. 1900	7	Connected to Shropshire & Shrewsbury Canals – had an inclined plane.
45	Shrewsbury	1796	c. 1921/ 1939		To LMSR 1922.
46	Montgomeryshire	1797	1936	18½	9 miles still navigable for pleasure boating.
47	Ellesmere Canal	1795/ c. 1820	Part used 1914/ 1938	88	Amalgamated 1813 to LMSR 1922.

48	Chester	1779	Part used	19¼	A 'Broad' Canal.
49	Trent & Mersey Canal	*c.* 1776	Used	93	Purchased by North Staffs Railway 1846. To LMSR 1922
50	Macclesfield	1831	Used	26	To LNER 1922
51	Uttoxeter	1811	*c.* 1847	13	
52a	Caldon	1779	Part used	17½	Part Trent and Mersey.
52b	Sir Nigel Gresley's Canal	1776	1857	3	From Appledale Collieries to Newcastle-under-Lyme.
53	Grand Trunk (see Trent & Mersey)				
54	Derby Canal (had the first iron trough aqueduct)	*c.* 1796	Part 1817 *c.* 1908	18	From Derby to Erewash Canal. Joined the Grand Trunk (the Act specified a toll-free amount of coal to be carried for the poor of Derby).
55	Trent Navigation	1773/1801	Part	94	
56a	Coventry Canal	1790	Part	33	Part Coal Board owned.
56b	Ashby-de-la-Zouch Canal	1804	Part 1944/ 1957	30	To Midland Railway 1846.
57	Llechryd Canal & River Teife				
58	Pen Clawdd	1814	1818	4	
59	Kymers Canal	1769	*c.* 1867		
60	Kidwelly & Llanelly	1816	*c.* 1867	9	Became Railway in 1865.
61	Early Ashburnhams	1796	?	1½	Not shown separately on map. A group of canals feeding to the coast between the Towey & Loughor rivers (Camarthen Bay).
61a	Pembrey	1824	1843	2	
	Bowsers Level				
	Vauxhall Canal				
	Wern	1795	*c.* 1810		
	Hopkins				
	General Ward's (Dafen)	1769	*c.* 1810	¾	
	General Ward's (Ypitty)	1787	1820	1	
61b	Glan-Y-Wern Canal	1790	*c.* 1910	3½	A feeder to the Tennant

62	Swansea Canal continued by Trewyddfa Canal	1798	1931	16	Feed from western side of the Tawe River. To GWR 1873.
63a	Neath Canal (Had 19 locks in 13 miles)	c. 1795	1934	14	Semi derelict at 1948 Nationalisation.
63b	Tennant Canal	1824	1934	5	
64	Aberdare Canal	1812	c. 1930	6	Feeder to the Glamorganshire Canal.
65	Glamorganshire	1798 1812	1945 1900	25½ 7	From Merthyr Tydfil to Cardiff.
66a	Monmouthshire (renamed Monmouthshire Railway & Canal Co.)	1799/1814	1849/1853	23	Became a railway.
66b	Breckock & Abergavenny	1812	c. 1933	33	Sold to GWR 1880.
67	Birmingham & Liverpool Junction	1835	Part used c. 1940	51	Leased to LNWR to 1922.
68					
69	Wyrely & Essington	1795/1859	Part used 1950s	48	British Waterways Board.
70	Birmingham & Fazeley	1789	In use	21	
71	Warwick & Birmingham (sec Grand Union)	1800	Part	22½	Purchased by Regents Canal 1929.
72	Warwick & Napton (see Grand Union)	1800	Part	15	Purchased by Regents Canal 1929.

Other Canals Not Shown On Diagrammatic Map

| Map | Canal | Commercial Use | | Length | Notes |
		Opened	Closed	Miles (to nearest)	
73	Par	1847	1855	2	
74	Brown's	1801	?	1	Branches from the River Brue.
75	Galton's	1805	1850	1½	Abandoned 1897.

76	Cyfartha	1776	1835	2	
76a	Doctor's	1813	c. 1910	1	
77	Llansamlett (Smith's) Canal	1784	1852	3	Feeding from the eastern side to the Tawe River.
78	Lydney	1813	Still open	1	
79	Penrhiwtyn	c. 1793	1798	½	Absorbed by Neath Canal Co.
80	Red Jacket	1790/1818	c. 1922	2	To join the Rivers Neath and Tawe.
81	Trewyddfa	1719	1931	1½	Continuation of the Swansea Canal.
82	Kilgetty Canal				West of Carmarthen Bay, north of Tenby.
83	Stourbridge Extension Canal	1849	1935 Part 1960	4	Bought by OWWR 1846 then GWR.
84	Sir John Glyn's	1776	1857	3	

Note 1
As with the Railways, there were a further number of canals which were proposed and authorised, but were, for various reasons, practical, economic or financial, not started.

Note 2
The closure of a canal required the issuing of a 'Closure Notice', followed (often some years later) by an 'Abandonment Order'.

Note 3
Portions of some canals are now still open, often maintained by private enthusiasts and for pleasure use. 'Preservation' societies exist in the same way as those groups which maintain resurrected steam (see 'Tailpiece' at end of book).

Note 4
Reference to Note 3, 'pleasure use'. In the early years, the only people allowed on the tow path were the official users of the canal. It was an 'offence' to trespass.

Note 5
The 'Notes' of the foregoing table of canals only really scratch the surface of the real stories behind the building and life of the canals listed. The range of books by Charles Hadfield give extensive detailed coverage

The note on the broad gauge/canal map on page 30 refers to the many canals in the Birmingham area in addition to the main waterways. The following table lists the branch canals, with basic known details. During their lifespan, some canals and branches were updated in width of lock, depth and course. The reference numbers on the following list are for identification only, they are NOT related to the canal map on page 30, and relate to the Birmingham area only.

Ref No.	Branch	Length miles	Opened	Abandoned	Ref No.	Branch	Length miles	Opened	Abandoned
1	Anglesey	1½	1850		31	Neachells	⅜	1845	1953
2	Anson	1⅜	1830	1956/61	32	Netherton Tunnel	2⅜	1838	1955
3	Ball's Hill				33	Newall	½	1772	1901/1948
4	Bilston	⅛		1953	34	Norton Springs	⅛	1888	
5	Birchills	2⅛	1798		35	Ocker Hill	⅛	1774	1955
6	Birmingham Heath	¼			36	Ocker Hill Tunnel	⅛	1805	
7	Bradley	⅜	1818	1955/9/61	37	Oldbury Loop	½		1957/60
8	Bradley Locks	⅝	1849	1961	38	Old Wharf	¼		
9	Bumble Hole	¼	1803	1960	39	Oozell's Street			
10	Causeway Green	½	1858	1954/9/60	40	Parker	⅛	1938/48	1953
11	Chemical Arm (Houghton)	¼			41	Pensnett	1¼	1840	
12	Church Bridge	⅝	1860	1955	42	Ridgacre	¾	1826	
13	Danks	½		1954/60	43	Rotton Park Loop			
14	Dartmouth	⅜	1828	1947	44	Short Heath	⅛	1798	1909
15	Daw End	5⅝	1800		45	Sneyd Locks			
16	Digbeth	1	1799		46	Soho			
17	Dixon	¾	1829	1954/65	47	Spon Lane Locks			
18	Dunkirk	⅛	1850	1953	48	Tipton Green Locks	¼	c. 1805	1960
19	Engine	⅜	1789		49	Titford	7⅞	1837	1960
20	Gibson's	⅛	1812	1920?	50	Toll End	1⅜	1809	
21	Gospel Oak	⅜	1800	1954	51	Two Lock Line			
22	Gower	½	1836		52	Union	⅛		1955
23	Graze Brook	⅛	1840	1953	53	Union (Roway)	¼		1955
24	Haines	⅜	1833		54	Walsall Locks	⅝	1841	
25	Halford	½	1828	1947	55	Willenhall	⅛	1803	1953
26	Izon	⅛		1954 Part	56	Withymoor	⅜	1858	1954
27	Izon Old Turn				57	Wyrley Bank	1½	1797	1954
28	Jesson	⅛	1831	1954	58	Essington Locks			
29	Lord Hay's	1¼	1800	1930	59	Cannock Extension		1778	
30	Monway	⅜	1812/13	1953	60	Lord Wards	⅛		

LONGER LENGTH CANALS								
Wednesbury	⅜	1769	1954/60		Walsall	7¼	1799	
Bentley	3⅜	1843	1961		Tame Valley	8½		
Birmingham & Fazely	20¾	1789						

Among the outstanding examples of canal engineering are the pumping stations that maintained water levels, always a problem in some canals. Two different examples which are still operating are the Crofton and the Claverton on the Kennet & Avon at its highest points. With the former, the 1807 pump station houses a Bolton & Watt engine built in 1812. With a 6-tonne beam, it is in excellent working order, used on 'steam days' (steam from Lancashire boiler) when electric pumps are switched off, and assisted by a Sims combined cylinders engine built by Harveys of Hayle in 1846. Both 'stand by' for emergencies. The Claverton pump (built 1810) is also beam operated and driven by a huge waterwheel turned by the River Avon. It worked for about 140 years and was restored 1978. Both of these are well worth a visit.

2

Plateways & Tramroads

Plateways and tramroads were initiated by many canals, or as separate lines in their own right, and it is surprising how complicated such a story can be, considering simple rails on stone blocks, and at what phase of development you happen to study.

Many of the lines went through numerous phases of development. Name changes are common, particularly when, as often happened, a track was extended to join another, and thus a combined name would result. To make things more complicated from a record point of view, often not only was the gauge of one or both altered, but the form of rail design also changed, say from 'plate' to 'edge' or in some cases a combination of both.

The name of the canal also looms large in the changes as the 'founder' of the track. An example detailed in the next pages, the Monmouthshire Canal & Navigation Company (itself renamed The Monmouthshire Railway & Canal Co.) initiated the Crumlin Tramroad, 1792. This joined the second (of two) Sirhowey Tramroad to a junction with the Beaufort Tramroad. With others owned by the Canal Company, the Crumlin was converted to a railway about 1850 and became a constituent of the Western Valleys Railway.

In stepped the Great Western in 1875 and the 'Western Valleys' became Great Western property in 1880, after a five-year period of 'Running Power' over the Western Valleys' tracks.

These forerunners of the railways, as we now know them, form a critically important aspect of sequence of railway history and development, a portent observed as early as 1801 when Dr James Anderson published a book titled *Recreations in Agriculture* in which rail lines and horse traction were proposed to run along the sides of turnpike roads, 'for heavy loads and fast lighter loads'. He proposed a track from London to Bath as a future project! At the time not taken seriously but the 1804 Locomotive of Richard Trevithick soon proved the potential.

Here then was the start of the true 'Railway' history, in cast-iron plates, or stone sleeper blocks carrying short cast-iron or wrought-iron rails of various shapes. In use long before the Great Western Railway was born, or even thought of! The railway engineers were in the making, experimenting and operating from the smithies and workshops of the collieries, quarries and canals.

A very strange anomaly occurred in the 'canal boom' years of the 1770s and 1790s, one which could have had far reaching effects, but was overlooked, possibly in the canal constructing enthusiasm, technology, and euphoria of the period, almost akin to the railway boom fifty years later.

There were already in existence a number of tramways and plateways, horse-drawn railways of a sort, on which trucks for coal or stone etc. ran on a slotted plate or on a simple cast-iron rail mounted on stone blocks. Tramways were quite widely used by canal companies either in construction of their waterways, or to join sections or locations where a canal was considered non viable because of terrain and construction difficulties.

Many tramways were used in the South Wales area, later closely related to the Great Western, due to just such terrain difficulties, linking the often almost inaccessible mines and quarries to canals and ports. The rights to construct these early rail systems were often included in the Acts which allowed construction of the canals. There was a restricting clause in the Acts which allowed tramroads up to about 8 miles from a canal. If a canal company refused, for whatever reason, to link say, a mine or quarry to a canal by tramroad, the mine or quarry owners could go ahead with arrangements to have a tramroad built. Some canal owners acceded willingly and enthusiastically with tramroad requests, but others flatly refused, seeing what they thought, rightly as it was proved, the thin end of the railway wedge.

A Note on Plateways and Tramroads

The following notes outline, and the accompanying list records the 'horse railways' which existed, most associated with canals, in the approximate area eventually covered by the tracks and influence of the Great Western Railway. The life of a tramroad or plateway relied almost exclusively on the viability of, at one end, the mine or quarry etc. which it served, and at the other end the canal to which it connected. Failure of either could render it useless.

Originally purely as mineral lines from source to accessible road or water, the increasing demand for more speed and capacity indicated the need for a much more powerful 'horse'! Communication was improving along with the roads, but even here capacity was becoming inadequate, and there was a need to develop a 'stage coach' with more space for more travellers, when passenger travel was added to the 'mineral' forerunner.

The Trevithick 'steam horse' of 1804, actually built for use on a tramroad, started the trend, developed in a quarrying, mining, iron-working area to provide the increased mobile power required. By the time George Stephenson produced his updated version of the mobile steam traction plant, the potential had been already opened up. The steam locomotive engine was the new power source, and the horse plateways and tramroads were becoming part of development history, as the steam application developed the horse was slowly phased out.

Individual histories were very varied. Changes of ownership, type of track, gauge of track, part closures and absorptions were common to plateways and tramroads, but closure, realignments, re-routings and conversions to standard 4-ft 8½-in gauge for the developed steam locomotive were also common occurrences when takeovers occurred as the railway network system grew, although some remained as horse lines. The struggle with railways which was to come later was not foreseen when the canals had the upper hand where carriage of goods and passengers was concerned. Had the entrepreneurs triggered acts to build railways or tramways assisted by canals instead of vice versa, history may have been changed that much sooner.

Was there a portent for the future from the Duke of Bridgwater (1736–1803)? The elderly founder father of the British commercial canal system is said to have stated, 'They (the canals) will last my time, but I see mischief in those damned tramroads!'

The Duke was not the only influential canal enthusiast to appreciate the potential of the tramway. In the late 1790s, the engineer Thomas Telford had recommended the spread of canals, both new and joint links between canals. Within five years he was to write 'Experience has now convinced us, that where the surfaces are rugged, or where it is difficult to obtain water for lockage ... where weight of produce is great in comparison to bulk...that in those cases, iron railways are in general preferable to canal navigation ... (railways) may be constructed in a much more expeditious manner ... at a comparatively modest expense.' He also emphasised that rails may be taken up and relocated, also at moderate expense, something which couldn't be done with a canal!

Tramroads are recorded even long before 'canal mania' arrived. The comparative ease with which a horse could draw a loaded wagon over a prepared track, when compared to a rutted road, was quite outstanding. The first tracks, referred to as 'Rayle Ways', date from the opening of the seventeenth century in the area of Nottingham and were installed by a colliery owner. Continuing throughout the century, various introductions of wooden rails spread among individual collieries (later improved by an iron strip along the top of the wood rails), and in 1695 the owner of a copper works, Sir Humphrey Mackworth, built such a wood rail line, the first in South Wales, to connect the waterway facilities at Neath, the beginnings of the most extensive system in the country.

Wood gave way to iron, whether slotted plates or 'rails on edge' (the latter design credited to William Jessop but there is no factual proof of this) and continued to spread. The potential of the rail or tramroad was early seen to be the answer to a 'National' transport problem. Ben Outram, a pioneer tramroad engineer, pre-empted the later steam railway controversy by proposing a standardised gauge of track. A paper presented in 1800 also proposed a national system, with a track gauge of 4 ft 2 in, whilst yet another paper suggested a publicly owned, national system with wagon bodies which could be transferred from 'road to rail', one of the earliest proposals for a form of 'containerisation'!

This idea had really great potential, but, probably due to technology of the period, and an off-putting first attempt failure, was not exploited. In essence, it was an Outram attempt to cut out load transfer from tram wagon to canal boat, and it is possibly with the design of raft that the scheme failed. Unless specifically designed, a 'raft' is not the easiest of waterborne transport either to load, or control when in motion. Had more thought and perseverance been applied it could have been an outstanding contribution to canal transport.

Improvements could also have been made in several other ways. Standardisation may have proved an incentive to introduction as gauges seemed to range between 1 ft 6 in and 5 ft, every mine, quarry or works complex sporting its own gauge, but the iron rails were really opening up potential. There were many, and varied, debates recorded in 'Hansard', the parliamentary record. During our disagreements with

Napoleonic France (nothing changes does it?) and with a government always on the lookout for more revenue in the form of taxes, a Bill was proposed to levy a duty on iron. A debate in the House on 9 May 1806 produced a very interesting exchange and comments. Mr Mordaunt (Warwickshire), regretted opposing 'measures of finance at this arduous period', but recorded strong objections to the measure 'which meant inevitably ... throw a gloom on the spirit of our manufacturers ... and to drive from bread very numerous classes of our industrious poor ... inflicting injurious effects on a large proportion of the inhabitants of Birmingham which I have the honour to represent.'

During the debate, Mr Curwen (Carlisle) said, 'It has been found desirable to abolish wooden railways for the purpose of substituting iron rails, an object which this tax must defeat.'

Mr Wilberforce (Yorkshire): 'It is a principle of taxation that no duty should press upon any article in its rude and early state ... for the tax on the feelings of the subject might be more galling than on his pocket. Application of the excise to any branch of commercial enterprise is to be regretted, but in this instance, will prove more than usually vexatious'. Anyone agreeing with the Bill would be remembered at the next election!

The invidious fact of governmental money-grabbing continues unabated. In the early years of steam traction, competition between road and rail led to the appointment of a 'committee to enquire into unequal rates of taxation on different modes of travelling'. The debate of 18 May 1837 contained the following gem. Mr Gillon (Linlithgow) stated, 'Steam as a motive power whether on, railways, rivers or on the sea is totally untaxed ... while the railway coach is altogether untaxed, the stage coach travelling on the high road is subjected to a payment of an annual licence duty of £5. The conductor of the railway coach pays no duty; the driver of the stage coach has to pay an annual duty of £1-5s-0d.' Needless to say, railway travel was not taxed, and how shipping under steam would have had a tax applied was not detailed, so the whole proposal died a natural death!

However, to return to tramroads and plateways. Why were they called tramroads? There is a theory that it is a word based on the name of the engineer, Ben Outram. Maybe! Another theory points in the direction of a Latin derivation from the word '*Trames*', a pathway. Who knows? In any case iron rails or plates set the scene for the railways as we know them today, the earliest *public* railway in this country being introduced by Act of 1801 as the surrey Iron Railway (closed 1846), a Croydon to Wandsworth link in place of a non-practical canal proposal.

The first Railway Act proper had been by the Revd R. Brandling who appears to have had a joint calling, religious and secular (expecting profit from both?). On one hand the Church and on the other a thriving colliery! The Act for this line in the Leeds area dates from 1758. In the early years, the tramroads were part and parcel of collieries, quarries or canals, being owned and run by the enterprises themselves for their own ends. This concept changed with the William Jessop engineered Surrey Iron Railway and the opening of the Stockton & Darlington line in 1835 really set the seal.

At this time the main feature of a land transport power system was the horse, singly or in multiples, and so the early tramroads were fashioned to accommodate this form of motive power. The horse tramroad did not immediately die out with the introduction of steam power, several being retained or even constructed, for various locally practical reasons well into the steam locomotive era, and lasting for many years. Among such lines is the Severn and Wye (1810 – steam from 1864), horse powered for fifty-four years.

During the late 1820s, the horse lines were still being promoted, two being the Avon & Gloucestershire and the Bristol & Gloucestershire. At this time steam was seen to be the future, and these two horse examples were among the last to be initiated with the horse in mind.

During the late 1700s, the wood railways were switching to iron rails, and there was probably not a mine or quarry in the country which did not have its internal 'tramway' system, with its external link to road or water. Although immortally linked to the railway and the steam locomotive, George Stephenson came to fame really much later, after a great deal of pioneering work with both track and steam locomotive had already been done. Much of the credit for the 'Railway' as we know it has really gone to, one could almost say, the wrong man, or at best possibly too much credit! His contemporaries have slipped to second place.

The early 'locomotive' engineers, who were really working in colliery workshops to perfect something better and more powerful than the horse, had followed Trevithick's Penydarren tramroad success in 1804. Blenkinsop's rack rail engine of 1811 was also a pioneering step in the 'perfection' of a continuing series in putting mobile steam to practical use.

Although inevitably overlapping into the 'steam' era, the early horse-powered railways and tramroads, whilst not a 'linked' system in themselves, were certainly on the map as early developments of eventually a 'national' transport system. To those pioneers must go a great deal of credit, which seems to be generally lacking, so taken are we by the rapid developments of and from the 1820s, and from the work of George Stephenson in particular.

There are over 1,500 miles of horse powered tramroads recorded in this country, almost a third of which were located in the mining and quarrying area of South Wales, much later and in 'modernised' condition to be included in the Great Western Railway environs, but in the early years the locations for and witnesses to the first experiments with steam traction.

The increasing weights carried, and the need for more substantial track, led to several solutions coupled to problems. The introduction of uniform gauge (4 ft 8½ in) for the edge rail systems of the railway proper, meant that hundreds of tracks, as well as the tramway steam locomotives themselves, did not fit the concept, which was being rapidly introduced. As an example several of the Monmouthshire Railway & Canal Company's tracks were re-laid with a different style of plateway which combined the edge and plate system, allowing the use of both existing and later designs of truck and power source.

Possibly the earliest work in Britain which details tramway equipment such as rails, trucks, winding drums and an early steam engine, is John Curtis's publication of 1797 titled *The Coal Viewer and Engine Builder's Practical Companion*. This comprehensive work includes material weights and sizes of steam engine components up to 70-inch-diameter cylinders. Chapters detail the construction of wagon winding drums and methods of opening doors underground to allow passage of wagons through the mine system. The winding drums were fitted with brakes to retard the speed of wagons.

The phraseology used to describe various components contains many words which we still use, but some the reader may not have heard before. Among the instructions are those for manufacturing 'Jinneys for conveying the corves', with all timber sizes and costs specified including the cost of the carpenter. The 'Jinneys' were winding drums, and the 'corves' the wagons. The latter were fully specified, including all wood and ironwork, the detail of the ironwork accompanied by instructions to the blacksmith. The construction of the boiler, engine house and all pipe-work and the 'Beam' all fully specified. An outstanding 'first' in the field of engineering design and recording.

Detailed designs for the tramplates include drawing for sleepers and all forms of tramplate for 'plain turn plates', 'plates for turning into benks or boards', and 'common plates' all in cast iron.

The above shows that the technical approach to 'Railways' was certainly receiving early attention. Mobile steam application could take it that big leap forward into Trevithick's steam loco world of 1804.

A list of tramroads and plateways associated with the Great Western area is included at the end of this chapter, and, whilst many were of only short, or comparatively short lengths, they are inextricably linked to the canal and navigation systems which they so ably supported, and were the signposts which pointed to the future of steam railways and the developments to date, often turned into railways in their own right.

With all of the developments, design of wagons, types of rail, sleepers or stone blocks etc, there was increasing concern, indeed an early 'Health and Safety' move, to ensure that wagons and rails were not deliberately overloaded. Thus various byelaws were to be enforced which included the registration of all wagons with positive identification of the owners. By the 1870s, some authorities had installed weighing facilities to ensure adherence to weight limits, and fines could be imposed for overloading which, of course being human nature, there was always the one who got away with it and finished by breaking a plate rail! Overloaded wagons (or even one loaded correctly) often with no or very inefficient braking, could run away on down grades and crush the horse! So often the horse was uncoupled and led down following the wagons. With a road type wagon with shafts, the horse could have a (probably limited), braking effect, but with chain draft on free running rails the animal was very vulnerable, with no braking effect at all, particularly on a relatively smooth running plate or edge rail track, being easily run over by a runaway wagon.

Drivers were required to pay tolls depending on weight and type of goods carried, the goods detailed on a 'waybill' which had to be presented to the toll collector, with fines paid by those who tried to avoid showing the bill or falsifying the details thereon.

Regarding weights, in 1801 the Surrey Iron Railway Co. obtained an Act to build a tramway. The presentation included details of 'horsepower', a strong horse being capable of drawing 2,000 pounds. An experiment quoted a horse, pulling without undue fatigue, on an iron rail track, an increasing load up to 55 tonnes. Starting with 3 tonnes, more stone loaded wagons were added as the experiment continued, a surprising total considering up to 2,000 pounds on a good level road, less than one ton.

Several maps of the early 1800s show unnamed tramroads and plateways prefixed with 'Old', possibly indicating abandoned routes from mines or quarries where, due to the technology of the time, the seams were no longer accessible and the enterprise closed.

The story of the 'tramroads' is much older than the canal boom of the late 1700s which brought it to the fore. Some very old prints and woodcuts originating in Europe show tramways and small wheeled tubs, pushed or pulled by manpower, at mines and quarries. One of the earliest prints from Germany is dated 1550.

The earliest illustration in Britain is probably that of the manpowered tramway at Prior Park, Bath, *c.* 1750 (No. 49 in the picture section).

The most prolific use of tramroads and plateways was in the iron, coal, and quarrying areas of South Wales, a Great Western area. The map includes composite details based on Priestley's maps of 1830.

The following is a list of the tramroads numbered on the map on the next page. A more detailed list follows on pages 48–58 giving more information on named tramroads and plateways, some not shown on the map, and those from other 'Great Western' areas.

Tramroads and Plateways in South Wales

1	Carmarthenshire	17	Coffins
2	Pembrey	18	Cefn Rhigos
3	Llonelly Dock	19	Taibach
4	Penchawdd	20	Llansamlet
5	Swansea and Oystermouth	21	Nant Mwrwg
6	Aberdulais	22	Cwmavon
7	Duffryn Llinvi	23	Cwmavon Works
8	Bridgend	24	Dowlais
9	Penydarren	25	Penderyn
10	Rumney	26	Pentyrch Forge
11	Sirhowy	27	Blaenavon
12	Ebbw Vale	28	Hay
13	Brynoer	29	Watton
14	Mamhilad	30	Rassa
15	Llanpihangel	31	Coalbrookvale
16	Grosmont	32	Hirwavn-Abernant

Over the years of their existence, plateways and tramroads were often combined, gauges changed, routes altered, types of rail changed e.g. plateway to edge rail, some even to standard 4-ft 8½-in gauge. The motive power also changed from horse to steam in many cases.

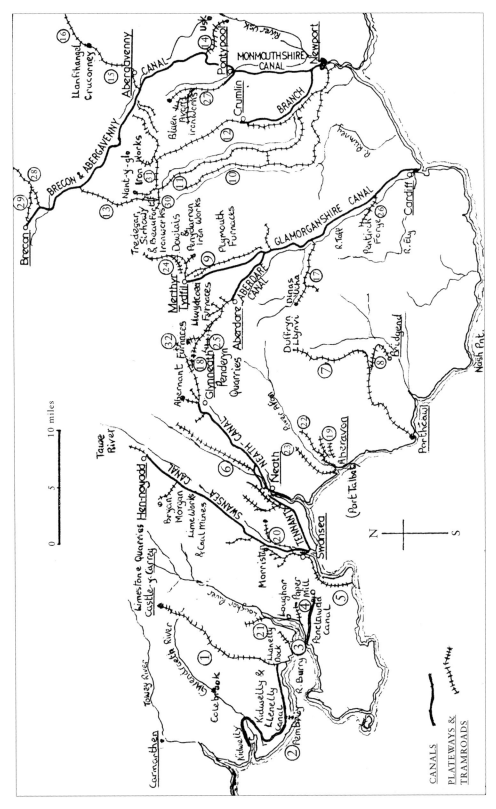

This sketch map shows the main named tramroads and plateways in South Wales. There are others, named and unnamed, which couldn't be included on a map of this size. See numbered lists following.

List of Plateways and Tramroads within the Approximate Area of the 'Great Western Railway'

A second number relates to the map on page 47. Cross-referenced to List One pages 110–26.

No. 1	No. 2	Details	Ref List 1
1		Monmouthshire Canal and its Railways (all closed, re-laid or converted to 4 ft 8 ½ in (from 3 ft 8 in) mineral lines *c.* 1853. Running Powers to GWR 1875. Absorbed by GWR 1880.	188
2	27	Blaenavon 5 ½ miles. Edge Rail 3 ft 4 in (1795) then plate 4 ft 2 in (1829). Steam tram engine from 1829. Incorporated 1792 by Monmouthshire Canal Navigation Co. Converted to a railway *c.* 1853. Absorbed by GWR 1880.	188
3		Abersycham from Blaenavon tramroad to ironworks, 1¾ miles 1827. Edge rail 3-ft 4-in gauge. Owned by canal.	
4	29	Varteg From Cwmavon to collieries 1½ miles 1819. Owned by canal.	188
5		Cwm Ffrwd From Blaenavon tramroad to Cwm Ffrwd. 2 miles. Plate 4-ft 2-in gauge. 1792 Part of Monmouth Railway & Canal Co. Renamed independent colliery transport system.	
6		Trosnant 1½ miles. From Pontypool to Pontymoile. Edge Rail 3-ft 1/4-in gauge rebuilt with plate 4-ft 2-in gauge 1803. Steam tram engine 1829.	
7		Blaen-Dare & Nant Ffwdoer Pontymoil to ironworks. 1 mile. 1796. Edge rail 3-ft 4-in gauge. Owned by canal. Steam tram engine 1829. Extended 3½ miles.	
8		Pontepool Pontnewydd to Trosnant line ¾ mile. 1829.	240
9		Caerleon Cwmbran to River Usk 4 miles, 1800. Extension to colliery.	
10		Nine Mile Point From Newport to Nine Mile Point 10 miles. Plate 4-ft 2-in gauge. Carried passengers from 1822. Used for tram engine steam experiments 1816–29. Part of Sirhowy Railway 1861.	
11		Old Rumney Bassaleg to Rhynmey Ironworks 23 miles, 1836. Plate track 4-ft 2-in gauge. Passengers from 1860. Steam tram engine 1840. Absorbed by Brecon & Merthyr Railway 1863, then to Great Western, 1922.	
12		Llanarth Tramroad 5 miles, 1824. Plate 4-ft 2-in gauge. Associated with:	
13	11	Sirhowy Tramroad No. 1 17 miles. 1802. Plate 4-ft 2-in gauge. Became Sirhowy Railway Company 1861. Passengers carried from 1822 and steam tram engine from 1829. Initiated by the Monmouthshire Canal Navigation Act. This was complicated by authorising Tramroad No. 2. No. 1 was a mineral horse drawn wagon way. Absorbed by the NNWR 1876. Running powers over No. 2 granted to the GWR 1875 and absorbed 1880. Converted to a Railway *c.* 1853. Included Crumlin Tramroad 1792.	188

14		Tredegar to quarries and ironworks. 5½ miles. 1805. For stone traffic. It was at the Tredegar Ironworks that Daniel Gooch started work as a moulder in the foundry. Steam tram engine from 1829. Rebuilt as a mineral line 1860.	
15		Cwmffwd Railroad Part built over by Monmouthshire Railway and Canal Company.	188
16		Rassa (or Raddau) to connect Sirhowy Ironworks, Beaufort Ironworks and Ebbw Vale line. 1794. Track edge rail 3-ft 4-in gauge re-laid as plate 4-ft 2-in gauge. Steam tram engine from 1829. (See also illustration 52 of the picture section.)	
17	30	Trevil Tramroad Company From Trevil Quarries to the Rassa line and Ebbw Vale Ironworks. 1797. Track plate 4-ft 2-in gauge.	
18	12	Ebbw Vale From canal at Crumlin to Beaufort Ironworks 9½ miles. 1796. Edge rail 3-ft 4-in gauge re-laid as plate 4-ft 2-in gauge.	
19	31	Colebrookvale From Aberbeeg to Coalbrookvale Ironworks 5½ miles. 1826. Steam tram engine from 1829.	
20		Morfords From Ebbw Vale Rolling Mills to Sirhowy Tramroad 3 miles. 1818. Closed 1839.	
21		Llanhilleth Crumlin Bridge to Cwm Cyffin 2 miles, 1799. Owned by Llanhilleth Coal Company.	
22		Hall's Tramroad (Abercarn Railway) From Cross Keys to Man Moel 7 miles. Opened c. 1810. Leased to the Ebbw Vale Ironworks 1853 for twenty years. 3-ft 0-in gauge. Part later leased to GWR in 1886.	2
ON THE RIVER USK:			
23		Somerton From Newport to quarries 1 mile. Opened c. 1808.	
24		Jack's Pill Short track to join river at Newport to Nine Mile Point tramroad.	
IN AREA OF BRECKNOCK & ABERGAVENNY CANAL:			
25		Craig-yr-Hafod From Llanover to quarries. Plate track 3-ft 0-in gauge.	
26	15	Llanvihangel Railway 6½ miles, 1814. Plate track 3-ft 6-in gauge. Joined Hereford Railway. Part abandoned 1846. Part absorbed by Monmouth Railway & Canal.	145 228
27	16	Grosmont Railway Extension of Llanvihangel Railway 7 miles. 1819. Plate track 3-ft 6-in gauge. Became part of Newport, Abergavenny & Hereford Railway 1846. Part Abandoned 1846.	145 228
28		Hill's* Tramroad Llanfoist to Ironworks 5 miles, 1825. Plate track 2-ft 0-in gauge. Closed before 1860.	
29		Pull-Du & Tyla Quarry In areas of Blaenavon Ironworks & quarries. 1815. Plate track	
30		Hill Pit*, Garn-yr-Erw 2-ft 0-in gauge. About 7 miles of linked tracks covering …	
31		Cwm Nant Ddu five plateways.	

---

* Hill's had one of the longest tunnels, about 1 mile long, built 1825.

ASSOCIATED WITH THE STRATFORD-ON-AVON CANAL:			
32		Stratford & Moreton Railway 16 miles, 1826. 4-ft 8½-in edge rails. Absorbed by Oxford, Worcester & Wolverhampton Railway 1852, and then West Midland 1860. Great Western 1863. General passenger traffic 1853. Abandoned 1869. 4-ft 8½-in track laid on tramway between Stratford-on-Avon & Moreton-in-Marsh. 'Fish bellied' rail on stone 'sleepers'. Taken up in 1918 (see illustration 56 of truck and rail). Also recorded as 4-ft 0-in gauge and originally elm 4 ft 2 in.	291
33		Wilmcote Tramroad 1½ miles. Stone traffic. Closed 1900.	
34		Warings Green Tramroad 2 miles to limestone quarries.	
ASSOCIATED WITH THE GLOUCESTER & BERKELEY CANAL:			
35		Gloucester & Cheltenham Railway From Gloucester to Cheltenham 9 miles. 1811. Plate track 3-ft 6-in gauge. Integrated with Birmingham & Gloucester Railway and Cheltenham & Great Western Union Railway. To GWR 1836. Closed as a tramway in 1859.	
36		Leckhampton Plateway Connected with Gloucester to Cheltenham Railway 3 miles. Owner Gloucester to Cheltenham. Plate 3-ft 6-in gauge. Stone traffic.	
ASSOCATED WITH THE RIVER AVON:			
37		Bristol & Gloucester Railway Harbour to coal pit heath 9 miles. 1833. 4-ft 8-in gauge. Absorbed by Midland Railway 1845. (Lost to Midland Railway in shares price wrangle 1845).	47
38		Avon & Gloucestershire Railway From Keynsham to Bristol & Railway near Mangotsfield 5¼ miles. 4-ft 8-in gauge fish bellied edge rail. Owned by Kennet & Avon Canal, then GWR 1851. Closed 1865.	14
ASSOCIATED WITH RIVERS SEVERN & WYE & FOREST OF DEAN COLLIERIES:			
39		Bullo Pill From dock to collieries 7 miles. 1809. Plate track 3-ft 6-in gauge. Taken over by Forest of Dean Railway 1826, then South Wales Railway 1849, which itself was taken over by the GWR in 1863 after a leasing period from 1852. (This line had the first 1,000-yd railway tunnel in the world 1809.) This route connected with the Severn. Within the triangle formed by Lydney, Newnham and Monmouth were a number of unnamed privately owned tramroads. Also in this group we could mention the Lydney and Lidbrook (became the Severn & Wye), and the Monmouth, as the two named routes. There were also about twelve branches which were ¾–2½ miles long and which stemmed from colliery development, interconnected to the Lydney and Lidbrook track and the Monmouth line.	
40		Monmouth Plateway 11 miles of line including branches of ½ mile (Tinplate Works) and 3 miles to collieries. Opened 1812. Plate 3-ft 6-in gauge. To Coleford Railway 1872, then GWR 1875. Track removed in 1880 by GWR.	
41		Lydney & Lidbrook became the:	269

42		Severn & Wye Railway 32 miles including numerous branches. 1810. Gauge plate 3 ft 6 in, then 3 ft 7 in (1840), then 3 ft 8 in (1843). Steam 1864. General spasmodic closure and absorption of sections from 1868. Associated with Lydney Harbour and Canal.	
EAST BANK OF THE WYE:			
43		Teagues Railway 3 miles. Opened 1801. Closed 1803.	
EAST BANK OF THE TAWE:			
44A		Llansamlet Old Wagon Way About 2½ miles. Opened 1743. Closed 1803.	
44B		Scotts Tramroad ½ mile. Opened 1820. Closed 1823. Coal traffic, Lower Lydbrook (see Llansamlet Tramroad).	
SOUTH BANK OF THE WYE:			
45		Hereford Railway Co. Joined Wye Bridge to Grosmont Railway 11 miles, 1829. Part absorbed by Newport, Hereford & Abergavenny Railway 1846 which was itself absorbed by the GWR 1863. General Traffic. Passengers from 1839.	211
46		Kington Railway (Extension of Hay Railway) 14 miles. 1820–25. 3-ft 6-in gauge. Became Kingston & Eardisley Railway *c.* 1863 when it absorbed the Kington Tramroad. Taken over by the GWR 1897.	147
ASSOCIATED WITH SOMERSET COAL CANAL:			
47		Radstock Railway Built over an original canal. About 9 miles. 1815. Plate track possibly 3-ft 3-in gauge. Owned by Somerset & Dorset Railway, which went to the LMS&SR 1923.	
48		Combe Hay (Where an inclined plane replaced an old Caisson lift.) Opened 1800, closed 1802.	
49		Paulton, Tyning & Timsbury About 3 miles of short lengths linking the canal. Plate track possibly 3-ft 6-in gauge.	
ASSOCIATED WITH THE RIVER AVON:			
50		Prior Park Wagonway at Combe Down From Bath Avon to Combe Down Quarries. 1731. An early wood track with a gauge of 3 ft 9 in. Track 1½ miles, with a drop of 500 ft. The owner's house, built of Bath stone, became a showpiece and boosted the use of the stone. The illustration (No. 19 in the picture section) is thought to be the earliest depicting a tramway in Britain, and is dated 1750. The rails were 5 ft wide by 6 ft deep, lengths of oak.	
51		Hampton Down Also wood track. 1724. For quarried stone traffic.	
IN DEVON:			
52		Buckfastleigh, Totnes & South Devon Railway Worked by horses until 1874. Integrated with Shrewsbury & Chester, and South Devon Railway, then GWR in 1876.	281
ASSOCIATED WITH THE STOVER CANAL:			
53		Haytor Granite Tramway From Ventiford Wharf to the granite quarries around 10 miles. Opened 1820. Track special granite blocks in 'L' section lengths with a 4-ft 3-in gauge. Blocks still there in some places, but closed in 1848.	

ASSOCIATED WITH THE RIVER PLYM:			
54		Plymouth & Dartmouth Railway Sutton Pool to Princetown 25 miles. Edge rail to 4-ft 6-in gauge. 1823, later owned by South Devon Railway (1851), then Princetown Railway (1878), the latter financed by the GWR, which took over in 1883. Parts being previously abandoned about 1878.	235
55		Cann Quarry Extension from Plymouth & Dartmoor Railway to the quarries 2 miles. Opened 1830. Edge rail 4-ft 6-in gauge.	
56		Zeal Tor Tramway From Peat Beds to Naptha Works at Shipley Bridge 3½ miles. Opened 1847. Wood rails on granite sleepers.	
57		Redlake Tramway To serve a china clay quarry 7½ miles. A very late 1911 tramway. One loco 0-4-2. Closed 1932 on the failure of the quarry.	
58		Devon Great Consols Tramway From Great Consols Mine to Morwhellam Quay 5 miles. 3-ft 0-in gauge. Three locos and sixty wagons. Opened 1859. Closed 1899 as part of the refurbishment of …	
58A		Morwhellam Quay as a tourist attraction. Possibly the last 'Tramway' built was that included in the recreation of the George & Charlotte mine environs, associated with the Quay, in 1978.	
ASSOCIATED WITH THE TAVISTOCK CANAL:			
59		Morwhellam With an inclined plane from canal to the Tamar, 1817, edge rail at 4-ft 3-in gauge. The plane incline was 1:6 and was operated by a water wheel.	
ASSOCIATED WITH THE BUDE CANAL:			
60		Bude Plateway From Bude Haven to the canal, very short length of track, less than ¼ mile. 1825. Plate track 4-ft 0-in gauge.	
61		Redruth & Chacewater Railway From Devoran to Redruth 10 miles. 1826. Edge rail to 4-ft 0-in gauge. Steam engines from 1854 and track rebuilt on stone blocks. Closed 1915. Remained independent of the GWR until closure. Abandoned 1918.	
62		Poldice Railway From Portreath to Poldice Mines 5 miles. Plate track to 3-ft 0-in gauge. Closed 1864.	
63		Pentewan Railway From Pentewan Quay to St Austell 4 miles. 1829. Edge rail 2-ft 6-in gauge. Passenger traffic from 1830. Rebuilt as a mineral line in 1873. Closed 1916.	
64		Pen Pee Quarry Newlyn. 2-ft 0-in gauge. Steam until 1940. Diesel from 1940 until 1972 when the whole line was replaced by a conveyor belt!	
65		Parknoweth From Pack Horse Road to Penzance on the tin mines 2½ miles.	
66		Treffry Tramroad From the area mines to Par Harbour, with 2 miles of canal, 1840. Privately owned but taken over by the Cornwall Minerals Railway in 1870, later absorbed by GWR after working under agreement from 1877 and eventually purchased in 1896. (See Illustration 59 and 60)	84

ASSOCIATED WITH THE ELLESMERE & CHESTER CANAL:			
67		Llangollen From Canal to quarries 4½ miles. 1852. Edge rail 3-ft 0-in gauge.	
68		Ruabon Brook From canals to collieries 3¼ miles. 1806	164
69		Fron Cysllte About 1½ miles in area to collieries and quarry.	
70		Black Park	
IN AREA:			
71		Bersham & Ponkey From Brymbo Hall to Glascoed Valley 2 miles. 1757. Opened by the Iron Master, John Wilkinson. For iron and iron stone transport to and from the furnaces.	239
IN CAERNARVONSHIRE:			
72		Penrhyn Railway Port Penrhyn to quarries at Bethesda 6¼ miles. 1801. Laid with Wyatt's design of oval section rail to 1-ft 11¼-in gauge. Closed and re-laid on an altered route as a mineral line in 1874. (Hunslet Loco gauge listed as 1-ft 10¾-in gauge.) Special trackwork allowed crossing over standard gauge track. Steam from c. 1880. All condemned c. 1965 and replaced by diesel lorries! Most locos by Hunslet, but some from various other makes.	
73		Dinorwic From port to quarries 5 miles. 1824. Edge rails to 4-ft 0-in gauge. Re-laid on an altered route as the Padarn Railway 1848. 4-ft 0-in gauge (Llanberis) nineteen Hunslett saddle tanks. Working to heights of 2,000 ft. Plus cable worked inclines from various levels. 1-ft 10¾-in gauge. The little trucks had double flange wheels.	
74		Nantle Railway From harbour to quarries 8½ miles, 1828. Edge rail 3-ft 6-in gauge. Part closure 1879, when part was incorporated in the Caernarvonshire Railway. The quarry section was not closed until 1963.	
IN MERIONETH:			
75		Traeth Mawr Portmadoc Harbour Causeway, about 1 mile. 1811. Watts' rail 3-ft 0-in gauge. Closed 1835 later part Ffestiniog.	
		Note: Two Railways, from early beginnings, have now become prominent in the Tourist Trade, and are specially mentioned as starting in the Pack Horse era, although one left it rather late to start. Following is a 'thumbnail sketch' of both.	
76A		The Talyllin Railway This company embraced the facets of the theme of this book. Started in 1847, a very difficult access to the quarry at Bryn Eglwys ensured that the early slate loads were transported by pack horses for shipment from Aberdovey. Change of ownership introduced plate rail track and horse-drawn wagons followed by. In 1865, two 0-4-0 saddle tank locos from Fletcher Jennings & Co. The quarry eventually closed but the owner retained a (loss making) passenger service until his death. Final closure occurred in 1947. Taken over by a Preservation Society in 1950 it is now a thriving tourist attraction.	

76B		Ffestiniog Railway This is another company which involved the pack horse, the horse plateway and the railway proper. Success followed the building, 1808–11 of a substantial sea wall (known as the 'Cob'), altering the nature of the area with the siting of a new harbour at Portmadoc. The horse tramway ran along the Cob for upward of twenty-five years. In 1832 a new railway of 1-ft 11½-in gauge was authorised. Around 14 miles. The designing engineer was followed in 1859 by his son, who ordered two o-4-o locomotives (against the arguments of Brunel and Stephenson who said 2-ft o-in gauge would not work with steam power. The double ended 'Fairlie' loco successfully introduced *c.* 1870. In 1939 the Ffestiniog closed for passenger traffic, and in 1946 was completely abandoned. Enthusiasts in the mid-1950s opened it up again, and the rest, as they say, is history!	121
ASSOCIATED WITH MONTGOMERYSHIRE CANAL:			
77		Welsh Pool Railroad Very short length, ½ mile, from Welshpool to quarry. 1818. Edge rail 3-ft o-in gauge. Closed 1850 and became part route of Welshpool & Llanfair Light Railway.	328
ASSOCIATED WITH BRECKNOCK & ABERGAVENNY CANAL:			
78	28	Hay Railway From canal to connect with the Kingston Railway (Eardisley) 24 miles. 1817. Plate track to 3-ft 6-in gauge. Closed in 1860 and part absorbed by the Hereford, Hay and Brecon Railway. Other companies were involved becoming the Brecon, Merthyr Tydfil Junction Railway in 1865. This was declared invalid and absorbed by the Midland Railway in 1874.	147
79	29	Walton Plateway From the Hay Railway into Brecon. About 1 mile. 1817. Plate track.	
80	13	Brynoer Tramroad From Tal-y-Bont to Rhymney Ironworks 12 miles, 1815. Plate track to 3-ft 6-in gauge. Closed 1865.	
81		Llangattock Crickhowell to canal 8 miles. 1820. Plate track later converted to edge rail, and extended 1825. Closed *c.* 1911.	
82		Glangrwyney From Basin to forge 1½ miles, 1794. Edge rail then converted to plate. Steam tram engine used. Closed 1908.	
83		Beaufort From canal to Beaufort 6 miles, 1795. Edge rail then plate. Finally rebuilt with edge rail track. Part closed 1860 remainder 1908. (The Beaufort and Glangrwyney tramroads were part of the Monmouthshire Railway and Canal Company. GWR running powers 1875. Absorbed 1880.	188
84		Llammarch From canal to mines and ironworks at Clydach. 1795. Plate Track.	
85		Bailey's Tramroad From Govilon to Brymawr 5½ miles. 1822. Plate track to 4-ft 4-in gauge. In 1859 became part of the Merthyr, Tredegar & Abergavenny Railway which itself was absorbed by the London North Western Railway in 1866.	180
ASSOCIATED WITH SWANSEA CANAL:			
86		Hen Newidd & Cribarth From end of canal to Cribarth Quarries 4½ miles. 1798. Plate track gauge.	
87		Gwain-Clawdd, Hendreladis & Cwm Giedd Three short tramroads, about 2 miles total. 1830–40. Plate track gauge.	
88		Claypons Tramroad From Ynysgedwyn to join Brecon Forest Tramroad 4 miles. 1834. To Neath & Brecon Railway 1867.	

89		Palleg Tramroad 1½ miles also from Ynysgedwyn to Palleg Colliery. Opened 1807.	
90		Brecon Forest Tramroad From Devynock to Drum Colliery 13 miles. 1825. Plate track 3-ft 6-in gauge. Part abandoned and part to Neath & Brecon Railway 1859.	207
91		Glovers Railway From Hirwaun to Penderyn Quarries 2 miles. 1786. Closed 1794.	
92 93 94		Gilwen, Ynysygeinon, Cwm-Du Wayb-y-Coed, Allt-Wen, Ynysymwnd Graigola, Ynys Tawe, Cwmdu All opened before 1830 and short tracks up to a mile or so long.	
95		Clydach From Clydach-on-Tawe to Craig Merthyr Collieries 3 miles. Edge rail 3-ft 6-in gauge. Later converted to mineral railway.	
96	5	Oystermouth Railway From Swansea Harbour to Castle Hill 7½ miles, 1806. Plate track 4-ft 0-in gauge, rebuilt to edge rail 1855. Carried passengers from 1807. Steam traction from 1877. Owned by Oystermouth Railway & Tramroad Co. (known as the Mumbles Railway). Included a branch 1½ miles towards Morriston. One of the earliest lines (as the Mumbles Railway) to be electrified.	
ASSOCIATED WITH NEATH CANAL:			
97	18	Cefn Rhigos From canal end to Hirwaun tramway 3¼ miles, 1805. Plate track 4-ft 2-in gauge. Closed 1819.	
98		Pont Nedd Fechan From Glyn Neath to Pwll Du-or-Byrrdiu 1¾ miles. Edge rail 2-ft 6-in gauge.	
99		Dinas 1½ miles to quarries, 1807. Plate track 4-ft 2-in gauge, then rebuilt about 1860 with a mixed gauge 2 ft 6 in and 3 ft 6 in.	
100 101		Cwm Derlwyn, Aberpergwm, Cwm Gwrach, Resolven, Tonna Short lengths of 1 mile or so to various collieries. Early 1800s	
102		Blaen-Cregan From Ponty-Coed to Blaen-Cregan Collieries 6 miles. Edge rail 3-ft 3-in gauge. Closed 1867.	
103		Clyne 2 miles to colliery at Cwm Blaen Palena.	
ASSOCIATED WITH CARDIFF CANAL (Glamorganshire Canal):			
104	24	Dowlais From end of canal to Dowlais Ironworks 1½ miles. 1793. Plate track to 4-ft 2½-in gauge. Joint ownership. Canal Company and Ironworks. During the 1830s a steam tram engine was introduced running on a rack rail track. Closed mid-1850s.	
105		Castle Morlais From Penydarren to Castle Morlais 2 miles, 1803. A mixed plate track of 4-ft 2-in and 2-ft 9½-in gauge. Owned by Dowlais Ironworks.	
106		Abercanaid, Gurnos Quarry Two short tracks both probably plate to 4-ft 2-in gauge. The latter owned by the Quarry Company and opened 1792.	
107	9	Penydarren From the canal to Penydarren Ironworks 9½ miles. 1802. Plate track at 4-ft 2-in gauge. This tramroad is what could be classed as the first steam railway in the world. Trevithick's experimental steam locomotive ran here in 1804, and showed that the days of the horse propelled tramroads were numbered (see also Illustration 66 of Tramway Plate and Illustration 3 of the 1804 locomotive).	

108 109	26	Llancaiach, Maor Mawr, Pentyrch Forge Three tracks each about 2½ miles long. All early 1800s, the first two to collieries and the latter to an ironworks.	
ASSOCIATED WITH THE ABERDARE CANAL:			
110	25	Penderyn Railway From Bryngwm Patch to Penderyn quarries 2 miles, 1794. 3-ft ½-in edge rail track later rebuilt with plate track to 3-ft 6-in gauge (1806). Owned by the canal.	
111	32	Hirwaun–Abernant Tramroad To Abernant Ironworks 4 miles. 1805. Plate track to 4-ft 2-in gauge. Owned by the canal. Steam tram engine from 1830. Closed 1900.	
112		Llwydcoed From end of canal to join Hirwaun–Abernant Tramroad 2 miles, 1811. Plate track to 4-ft 2-in gauge. Closed 1900.	
113 114		Gadlys Furnace, Abernant South, Abergwawr All less than 1 mile long. The first from the above tramroad to the ironworks, 1811. The second to Abernant Ironworks, and the last to a colliery.	
115	17	Gyfeillon & Dinas Uchaf (Dr Griffiths' Canal) From the end of the canal to Hafod Colliery 3¼ miles. 1809. Plate track 3-ft 0-in gauge. Closed 1914 with an extension to a colliery about 2 miles further on (1812) with the same plate track gauge.	
ASSOCIATED WITH PORTHCAWL HARBOUR:			
116	7	Duffryn Llinvi & Porthcawl Railway From the harbour to Duffryn Llini 17 miles, 1828. Edge rail track to 4-ft 7-in gauge. Became the Llinvi Valley Railway 1847 and then the South Wales Railway 1855, which was leased to the GWR in 1855 and absorbed by the GWR 1867.	169 103 221 284
117	18	Bridgend Railway Bridgend to connect to Duffryn Llinvi & Porthcawl Railway at Tondu, 1830. Edge rail track to 4-ft 7-in gauge. Later owned by Llinvi Valley Railway (1854) and then GWR.	169
118	23	Cwmavon Works From Morfa Newydd to tinplate works and on to Bryn Colliery 5 miles, 1819.	
119	22	Cwmavon From Abervan to Cwmavon 3 miles.	
ASSOCIATED WITH RIVER NEATH AND NEATH CANAL:			
120		Melyn Works This was Sir Humphrey Mackworth's railway. Wood track (1698) to copper and lead works and on to his colliery. Closed 1705.	
121		Llamsamlett Wagonway 2 miles. This was a wood track line dating from 1743 and altered into a canal (Llamsamlett Canal) in 1803.	
122		Llamsamlett Tramroad From River Tawe to colliery about 3 miles, 1816. Also known as Scott's Railway. Opened 1816, closed *c.* 1860.	
123		Waunarllwydd From Penclawdd Canal to colliery 1 mile.	
124		Tondu Brickworks *c.* 1750. 3 miles of track to brickworks.	
125	19	Taibach Waggonway Wood track to Taibach Works, Aberavon.	
126		Pont-Rhyd-y-fen From Cwmavon to Rhyd-y-fen blast furnaces 2 miles, 1824. Taken over by Rhondda & Swansea Bay Railway 1883, then GWR 1906. Steam engine from 1845.	

ASSOCIATED WITH RIVER LOUGHOR:			
127	21	Nant Mwrwg Llangennech to St David's Colliery 2 miles, 1833.	
ASSOCIATED WITH BURRY RIVER:			
128	3	Llanelly Railway From Machynys Pool to St David's Colliery 2¼ miles. Owned by Llanelly Railroad & Dock Company (1828) then GWR in 1873. Closed nominally and converted to a mineral railway.	63
129		Pencoed Railway From Machynys Pool to Pencoed Colliery 3 miles. Closed when pit closed in 1912.	
130		Wern Tramroad & Box Tramway Both from Wern Canal to collieries, about 2 miles total.	
131 132	1	Carmarthenshire Railway & Pwll Tramroad 15 miles from Llanelly (1805) to lime works. Edge rail. Tramroad 1½ miles to Pwll Colliery, 1826. Both owned by Carmarthenshire Railway or Tramroad Company.	62
133 134		Stanley Pit Tramroad & Garscwm From Pembrey Harbour to Pembrey Pit, about 1 mile, 1819. Also Pembrey Harbour to Garscwm Furnaces.	
ASSOCIATED WITH KIDWELLY & LLANELLY CANAL:			
135	2	Cwm Mawr This 1¼-mile tramroad continued along a section of the canal which was not completed, to collieries which owned it.	
136 137 138		New Lodge, Trimsaran & Carway Three short lengths totalling about 4½ miles from the canal to the quarries and collieries. All owned by the Canal Company. Eventually converting from a canal to a railway in 1865 and merging with burry Port & Gwendraeth Vallcy Railway (the BP&GV Railway was taken over by the GWR in 1822).	
139		Coygon Quarries 1¾ miles from the Taf River to Quarries, 1832.	
ASSOCATED WITH SANDERSFOOT HARBOUR:			
140		Saundersfoot Railway From the Harbour to anthracite collieries around 5 miles, 1832. Edge rail track to 4-ft ⅜-in gauge.	
141		Wiseman's Bridge Tramroad About 2½ miles. Also from the harbour to serve collieries and ironworks, 1842. Fish-bellied edge rail track to 4-ft ⅜-in gauge. Rebuilt as a mineral line in 1874.	

IN BERKSHIRE:			
142		Wantage Tramway This rather late 'tramway' built in 1875 connected the town of Wantage to the Great Western main London–Bristol line. For a short period, horses were used, and for some months in 1880 the use of two Mékarski patent compressed air locomotives was attempted with a special 'charging' building constructed, but the venture was not successful. The line was about 2½ miles long and closed 31 July 1925. It was powered, on the exit of the Mékarski locomotives, by small 0-4-0 locos, one of which is now preserved at Didcot GW Society shops. This was Loco No. 5, built in 1857 by George England Co. of Hatcham London and it started life on the Sandy & Potton Railway, Bedfordshire. The Sandy & Potton was absorbed fifteen years. Sold to the Wantage Company during 1878 and named Shannon, it lasted the life of the line and was then 'preserved' on a plinth at Wantage main line station. It was rescued and refurbished in the Swindon Works about 1947 and is fortunately still with us. (The author remembers seeing this loco in Swindon Works when he was an apprentice about sixty years ago. The loco is now on display at the GWS Works at Didcot.) There were other locomotives, two conventional 0-4-0s, a Manning Wardle Co. of 1888 and a GWR saddle tank, the latter an 1874 convertible from broad gauge which worked until being very badly damaged in an accident in 1919 when it was scrapped. Two other locomotives were steam tram engines, one to the 1879 Matthew's patent built by, possibly, Fox Walker & Co., and the other by Hughes & Co. of Loughborough, the latter firm becoming Brush Electric Co. in later years.	

Author's Note

Reference to 'Plateways' has retained a legacy in the term 'Plate Layer' for those working on even the modern railway system track. My great-grandfather began his career in 1849 on the Great Western, starting at the age of thirteen and coming from a family working on the Oxford Canal. My grandfather's birth certificate, dated 1861, records his father's occupation as 'Plate Layer'.

Tramways Associated Directly with the GWR and the Ironstone Lodes Of Oxfordshire

In the preceding list we briefly looked at those well-known locations where tramways feed direct to canals and waterways. A lesser-known area far inland also used tramways, some very late in the steam saga, to connect directly to the vicinity of Great Western Railway sidings, from where loads were transhipped for country-wide delivery.

Other main ironstone areas are of course outside the scope of this book, but most ironstone was transported via tramway and mainline railway and not by the canal system, which for later tramway developments had long gone.

No.	Details	
143	FAWLER	Opened 1858 to connect to the Oswestry, Worcester and Wolverhampton Railway. Gauge not known. Initially manual power and closed in 1866. Reopened again in 1880 as a horse tramway to 2-ft 3-in gauge, edge rail. Closed in 1886.
144	EAST ADDERBURY	Opened *c.* 1859 to connect to the GWR. Gauge 2-ft 0-in edge rail. Horse powered initially, later steam loco, about 1 mile. Opened to exploit ironstone deposits and closed on exhaustion of those deposits *c.* 1900.
145	WEST ADDERBURY	Opened 1890 to connect with the Banbury & Cheltenham Direct Railway. 1-ft 8-in gauge edge rail. One 0-4-0 side tank loco, which was not too successful due to the gradients involved. Horses also used. Closed 1922. An attempt to reopen *c.* 1930 lasted until 1939 when business finally closed.
146	NELL BRIDGE QUARRIES	Opened in area *c.* 1860 to connect to GWR. Tramway from *c.* 1870. 2-ft ?-in gauge edge rail. Length about ⅓ mile, closed 1874.
147	ASTROP MINES	Opened 1897. 2-ft 0-in gauge edge rail. Cable hauled trucks. Up to 2 miles of track as pits developed. Power was by horses up to the cable track, the latter powered by a stationary steam engine. Closed 1925.
148	MILTON PITS	Opened 1918 due to pressures for war production. 4-ft 8½-in gauge flat-bottomed edge track on plate chairs. 1½ miles to the GWR line. Four 0-6-0 side tank locos, three new and one dating from 1885. Closed 1921 after the war boom, reopened later until final closure in 1929.
149	BLOXHAM PITS	Opened 1918. 4-ft 8½-in gauge track flat-bottomed rail on sleepers. Steam locos and then petrol/electric from 1929. Two steam (0-6-0 and 0-4-0). Closed during the Second World War (1939–45) and opened again 1947. Closed 1954.
150	HOOK NORTON QUARRIES	Opened 1889 4-ft 8½-in and a 1-ft 8-in section. One standard gauge 0-6-0 tank loco and one 1-ft 8-in 0-4-0 tank loco. Total length almost 1 mile. Closed 1904.
151	BRYMBO QUARRIES	Opened 1896. 2-ft 0-in gauge edge rail. Eventually five locos; two 0-4-2 ST, 4-6-0 T, 2-6-2 T, 0-4-0 ST. The 4-6-0 ex-ROD was, as with the Sydenham Pits loco, too big, and the 2-6-2 also caused problems. The quarry's workshop carried out all maintenance including heavy repairs. A downturn after Second World War caused closure in 1946.
152	EARL OF DUDLEY'S QUARRIES	Opened *c.* 1900. 2-ft ?-in gauge with rope haulage, using twin track and counterbalancing full and empty wagons. Rather spasmodic operation and closure in 1916.

153	BYFIELD QUARRIES	Opened 1915. Standard gauge, flat bottomed. Very steep gradients. Nine locomotives, one o-4-o ST and eight o-6-o ST.
154	CHARWELTON QUARRIES	Opened c. 1917. 4-ft 8-in chaired and flat bottom rail. Closed 1933. Reopened 1941 and closed 1945. Reopened yet again 1951. Two o-4-o ST and four o-6-o ST.
155	OXFORDSHIRE IRONSTONE QUARRIES	Opened, as with a number of others, due to war demand in the First World War, the 4-ft 8½-in gauge track to the GWR line laid by prisoners of war. The war was over before production proper started. An extensive undertaking with many 'full size' railway facilities. A locomotive repair shop built in 1958 as an example, and a mix of flat bottom and chaired rail. Signal boxes and associated signals are also a feature. A total of about 10 miles of track, some double. The various loco makers undertook the heaviest of repair requirements to the locos. Thirty-one in number and o-4-o and o-6-o tanks.
160	EDGE HILL QUARRIES	Opened 1922, closed 1925. This is more the sad story of a light railway about 12 miles long than of a quarrying enterprise, all assisted by a cable section. The light railway and all its equipment was allowed to rot *in situ* until official closure in 1957, when it was thus too late to be of any use to anybody. The locos, two o-6-o T and a o-4-o tank, scrapped in 1946.
161	BURTON DASSETT QUARRIES	Opened 1868. Closed 1873. Reopened 1895. 2-ft o-in gauge ½-mile horse-powered tramway installed. Closed 1909. Reopened yet again in 1918, closing finally 1921. A one period transport by road to the GWR station at Fenny Compton. The whole abandoned and demolished 1929.
162	SYDENHAM IRONSTONE QUARRIES	Near Banbury. 2-ft o-in gauge. Three Andrew Barclay o-6-o tank locos from 1915, 1918 and 1919. Closed 1925 and, like many railway areas, now a business park.

This section has shown in outline the part played by the forerunners of the 'Railway' proper; the plateways and tramroads which proved the viability of the steam locomotive and the use of iron tracks, development of the latter shown in the picture section. It should be noted that whilst cast-iron rails and plates were used into the steam loco era until the 1830s, wrought or malleable iron rails were introduced in various shapes (as opposed to narrow rectangular section bars) from about 1808. By around 1820 various shapes were in vogue, shapes with broad top faces, the early narrow rectangular designs rapidly wearing grooves in the wheels which ran upon them. Lengths of rolled rail varied from 9–18 ft lengths.

The Rails
Early Experiments with 'Permanent Way' Design from the Mid-Nineteenth Century (The Continuing Quest for a Really Permanent Way)

Following on the heels of the tramroads and plateways with their great variations in gauges, different types of sleepers, of stone blocks or wood with 3-ft-long cast-iron plates and wood strip topped with iron strip rails, came the realisation that the rail and the wheel of whatever ran on it, whether coal tubs or steam locomotives, both wheel and rail were interdependent. Thus by the mid-1800s, rail design was taxing the ingenuity of railway engineers wherever railways existed, so much so that on 10 February 1852 Mr W. Adams presented a paper on the subject to the Institution of Civil Engineers. The 'Civils' at this time established, with the 'Mechanicals' in close pursuit!

It is interesting to speculate that this was the beginning of the technical disagreements which have existed, almost one could say to the present day, between the civil engineer and the mechanical or locomotive engineer. The Civils' insistence that locomotives were deliberately made too heavy for the track and allied structures; the mechanicals that track and structures were never made strong enough for the locomotives! So the arguments rumbled on for 150 years! And will probably continue, each accusing the other of thwarting their efforts.

The term 'permanent way' applied to the rail system means just that, but in the early years it was often anything but. The permanent way as such was governed of necessity by the materials available in the area or even country. Wrought-iron rails were succeeding cast-iron plates and the arguments raged on the design of such rails. Rails were supported on wood or stone or even shaped to be sunk into the ballast. The ballast itself varied per location or area. Crushed stone, burnt clay, sand, gravel, all with differing properties and all required to support railway lines, stability governed by many factors including designs to support any/all rolling stock to run on them. How wide should a rail be on its wearing surface? The narrower the rail the easier it grooved the wheels. Long rails expand and contract according to the weather. This must also be accommodated. Rails must absorb the running load over them without being crushed down into the ballast, but be resilient enough to 'bounce' back up when the load has passed. Such resilience must not allow the rail/sleeper combination of whatever form to disturb and thence destroy its security in the ballast itself. Such then were permanent way problems, understood from very early in the locomotive development saga.

As train speeds and weights increased, the simple rails of the mine and quarry tramroads and horse-drawn speeds and weights were no longer adequate although of the cheapest form. This was realised quickly in the long-distance American pioneer railroads where rails often curled up at the ends and ripped into the floor of passenger cars. This rail was the flat tire-bar design, directly spiked to longitudinal rough-sawn wood bulk sleepers, quickly abandoned as knowledge was gained from experience.

The year 1820 saw the patent of Mr Birkinshaw for a 'T' section, fish-bellied rail ranging from 28–35lb/yd, used quite extensively by George Stephenson for the Liverpool and Manchester Railway *c.* 1830. This rail was almost theoretically correct, but was abandoned quite quickly when it was found that fish belly shapes between the supporting sleepers did not allow the sleeper portion of the rail to recover from the train weight. It just bent at the sleepers and stayed bent.

The fish belly form gave way around 1833 to a parallel 'T' section rail which had a cast iron chair location and had a measure of success credited to Mr Vignoles. This was further developed by Mr Locke on the Grand Junction Railway a couple of years later, in the form of an 'H' section on its side. Mr Locke then undertook a series of investigations into rail form, suitable chairs and sleeper designs. The rail was 4½ in deep in the web with top and bottom bearing surfaces 2½ in wide, weighing in at 62lb/yd. The rails were secured in cast-iron chairs by compressed oak plugs and metal filler pieces which, from the jaw of the chair locked-in the web of the rail. This rail had a rather short life.

The inevitable use of the upside down 'T', spiked directly onto the sleepers (almost a modern concept), came into fashion. Known as the 'Stephenson and Vignoles Rail', it was used quite extensively in the USA, but rushed or badly maintained spiking led to accidents. Problems with the joint between two rail ends were a continuing concern in all rail designs, and numerous methods of support evolved. Rails rolled in two pieces to lock over one another were tried, giving a longitudinal scarf joint to avoid the rail end problem, but costly to make. During 1838, I. K. Brunel introduced the 'Bridge' rail to the Great Western, a design which was taken up generally by other railways. This hollow flat bottomed design had a more elaborate rival in the 'Barlow' saddleback rail. Used without sleepers, it bore in and on the ballast, and was riveted to bearers. This rail was apparently noisy in use, and was obviously hollow; the intended ballast support rarely filled, and thus supported, the hollow rail internal section.

During this mid-century period there was also controversy over the form and material used for sleepers. The stone blocks of the plateways and tramroads were by now mostly abandoned, but advocates still argued that they were better than longitudinal or transverse wooden sleepers, as they couldn't rot and could be set in ballast or normal soil. Stone blocks gave a hard, noisy ride and the 'for' and 'against' argument was finally solved by an experiment on the Leeds & Manchester line, a portion of which ran over a bed of solid rock. This was levelled, and the rails and chairs laid as they would have been on stone blocks. This track proved to be so hard and rigid that it was not possible to continue to use it, as just rails to rock, with no resilience at all. Experimenting on a similar theory, Mr Jesse Hartley laid track on walls of masonry in place of sleepers, the walls again being too rigid, the masonry soon crumbled and broke up. By the mid-century, rail lengths were increasing from 12–15 ft to 21 ft, and the recognition of a requirement of resilience in track beds led to extended use of wood for sleepers. Even here there were problems. Various woods were tried with varying results. Strength was a factor as was durability, and both chemical and 'coal oil' (creosote) were tried, the latter under pressure, and a system evolved which was to last till the end of the wood sleeper and the steam locomotive, when reinforced concrete or steel, became the norm. The springiness of wood sleepers was early noted, and the need to continually check and repack them became a routine maintenance chore.

Costs of the stone block system, and the maintenance and replacement of wood sleepers, led to experiments with metal sleepers. Having problems with durability of wood, Mr Reynolds introduced wood-lined cast-iron troughs, and a follow-on in 1846 Mr Greaves of Manchester and Mr Douglas combined ideas in the form of, by the former, a semi-spherical cast iron 'bowl' on which was mounted a chair designed by the latter. The half sphere rested on the surface, and could be replaced by means of two holes and a pointed rammer, the holes accessible on top of the 'bowl'. Used on the Egyptian Railway, it was found that rolling movement of the train forced the soft soil up through the two holes! So back to the drawing board!

Mr P. W. Barlow of the South Eastern Railway proposed a cast iron sleeper, during 1849, being a 3-ft-long plate with two half chair heads cast upon it, various bolts securing the rail in the chair. An improvement was introduced by Mr William H. Barlow following this pattern but casting with a complete chair, the rail to be gripped by a wood key driven in. We are now approaching the system with which most railway enthusiasts and veterans will be familiar! Apart from the continuing experiments with the sleeper, the chair, wood key and Bull Head rail had arrived.

Earlier, around 1833, a prize of £100 was offered for the best rail-securing system, and whilst no one system was approved, the embryo system made its appearance, so that by the mid-century, after experimenting with various sizes, the cast-iron chair and wood key came out top of this list. So, having solved the securing of rail to chair, the next vexing question was how to solve the blow of a rotating wheel, approaching, crossing and leaving a joint between two rails.

A first attempt to solve the problem was on the Blackwall Railway, when rails with scarfed ends were used, the ends dovetailed and forced into a chair. The line was a rope operated system so speed and hammering were not a problem, but someone had attempted a solution. There were many attempts which all included a special design of chair supported by a sleeper, but in 1849 on the Eastern Counties Railway the solution with which we are all familiar came about. Following experiments, the four-bolt 'fish plate' system was applied successfully, where the rail joint itself is 'freestanding' and is in the space between two sleepers. The system spread rapidly, the London North Western, the Midland, and the Eastern Counties adopting it.

Still experiments continued, one of the (possibly) most questionable was that of Mr R. Norris of Warrington who introduced in 1852 a joint chair actually cast *in situ* around the rail ends from metal prepared in a portable cupola. The really solid joint 'works most satisfactorily' according to the report. In 1852, on site, it must have been rather costly and particularly hazardous (no health and safety problems then). This reminds the author of the 'Thermit' welding process witnessed onsite for rail repair during the 1960s.

Mid-century *c.* 1854, the Barlow Rail was in full use (see Illustration 19). So, how do you put a fish plate on a Barlow rail? And how do you make a more durable rail. To answer the second question first, we are approaching bulk steel production, thanks to Mr Besserer and his 'converter', and in the words of the paper of Mr Adams referred to in the opening of these notes, 'If it be resolved to continue the use of inflexible girder rails, one of two methods must be resorted to. The first is to make the rail of steel, or to steel the surfaces, and the other is to increase the width.' He then goes into a technical argument on the joining of Barlow rail lengths. This was now resolved by introducing a 2½-ft-long 'saddle', like a Barlow rail in shape and fitting closely the under or inside surface of rail itself to which it was securely riveted (used by Brunel on the West Cornwall Railway).

By March 1854 yet another rail design was being recommended. This was Mr Adams' modified 'Girder' rail. Again used without sleepers directly onto the ballast, it weighed 92lb/yd. The wide 14-inch flat section sat firmly on the ballast and the downward vertical web held it against lateral movement. Adams also introduced variations of girder rail, supported by cross sleepers and the 'fish plates' buried in the ballast. There were two versions, differing only in size, design being the same and weighing 42 and 62lb/yd respectively.

There were many variations of jointing chairs and fish plates extant in the mid-century period. Messrs Fowler, Bell, Norris, Samuel etc. all came up with variations and methods, from Fowler's massive double chair to Samuel's combined joint chair and fish plate; Adams' had even proposed a bull head rail supported by clamping wood 'chairs' spiked to sleepers. A problem which came to light when the bull head rail was used with cast-iron chairs was that the theoretical turning over of the rail when worn, to use the similar underside as the running surface, did not work in practice.

The hammering the rail received 'bouncing' on its chair during the wearing down of the running surface had so damaged the underside of the wrought-iron rail that turning over exposed a very damaged and therefore unusable running surface.

At this stage of development, certain practical aspects of rail, chair, and sleeper design were later to be adopted, possibly with improvements, by all railway companies. The bull head rail chair and wood key mounted on wood transverse sleepers, (although in the illustration shows triangular form). Rectangular sleepers are those we all now recognise from the steam age right through to the end of the steam era, the familiar 'clickety-click' over the rail joints smoothed out in the march of progress.

One further worry must be mentioned, that of track drainage. Several engineers had noted the oozing water and sand particles pushed out by the moving train as the sleeper or rail flexed, and emphasis was being placed, including several impractical and costly sleeper and rail designs, to satisfactorily drain the track bed and ballast, including metal sleepers with drain tubes, and bolting perforated metal plates to webs rolled under the rail.

As Mr Adams' paper said at its end, 'It is clear that 'permanent way' is not yet finally permanent, by any known process, and if new processes are not to be proved there can be no chance of improvement.'

Have we still to reach that ideal? Experiments continue! But with the modern trend of concrete sleepers and flat bottom rails, are we going backwards into the 'stone block' era or its equivalent?

To conclude this look at the relevance of canals, plateways and tramroads in the development of the railway system, we should first acknowledge, strange though it may seem on the surface, the debt owed by the railways to the canal pioneers. We cannot know the great detail of the true effects on all areas with regard to the changes wrought on commercial and industrial bases, and on personal local failures and prosperities, but we can acknowledge the seeds sown with regard to expanded communications. The early plate and tramway 'railways', the development and growth of the 'contract' engineer, both civil and mechanical, and the hidden financial aspects of money investment potential and manipulation all combine in an explosion of economic expansion, speeding communication; drawing together the many differing communities of this island of ours, seemingly shortening distances between the growing industries of the country. In this race, the baton had been passed to the steam railway to progress even further and faster.

An Ingenious Use of Tram Track

In this section we have looked at tram, truck, and rail development but there was one other probably unique adaption on the tracks above Llanod from the Craig Ddu slate quarry, a high Ffestiniog site. There were two parallel narrow gauge tracks for the slate wagons, controlled by a central cable arrangement, loaded trucks going down and hauling up empties or with quarry men as passengers. The two tracks had a 3-ft space between them and were about 1,800 yds long and dropped in stages about 1,040 ft.

During the 1870s, a very inventive blacksmith at the quarry made a form of simple trolley on an iron frame with a seat about 2 ft by 8 in wide. One end of the board was fitted with a double flanged wheel at the front and a V-shaped iron heel at the back. From the iron frame under the seat, a bar with a flanged roller on the back of the seat board stretched across the gap between and resting on the two inner rail tracks which were 3 ft apart.

The assembly was called the 'car gwyllt' or 'wild car'. Eventually each quarryman had his own car gwyllt, and there is a photograph of a convoy of cars with the men seated, feet stretched out in front of them *en route* down the tracks when the shift ended. The angle of the slopes was not too steep and the journey could be completed in about eight minutes, a simple brake lever acting on the front wheels. It certainly shortened the long walk home or in later years in time for the bus.

The quarry closed in 1939 but reopened for a short time after the Second World War, the slate used for London bomb damage repairs. What the present 'elf and safety' people would have made of the 'car gwyllt' I leave to the imagination of the reader.

1. 'On the Coach Road to Bath.'

2. The pack horse track.

3. Opening of the Stockton & Darlington Line.

4. Boat lifts formerly in use on Grand Western Canal.

Above and below: 5 & 6. Crofton Pumphouse. Great Western influence is prominent on various fittings. 'GWR Makers, Swindon Works' is clearly seen on the fire hole doors surround on the 'Lancashire' type boiler.

7 & 8. The 'business ends' of the 6-tonne cast-iron beam, showing piston and pump rods (in all beam engine pump houses, the cylinder end mechanism was polished, the pump ends greased).

9. The Main Entrance to Crofton pumphouse.

10. Inside the pumphouse.

11. Example of a vertical lift, one of those pieces of canal engineering used to raise a complete vessel from one level of water to another. Fortunately nothing like this was required for the steam locomotive. This is the Anderton Lift on the Weaver Navigation.

12. An example of one of the largest 'Inclined Planes' – as with the above lift – used for raising vessels from one level to another. Both this and the above example show part of the facet of Canal Engineering adding greatly to the costs. Note the boats in the carriages.

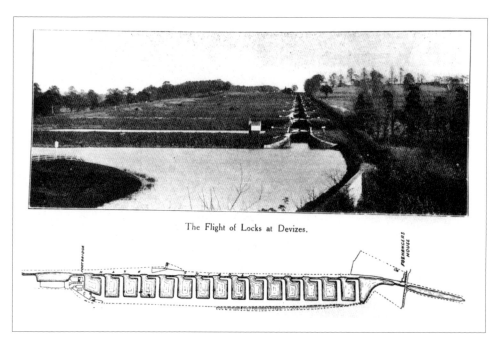

The Flight of Locks at Devizes.

13. Part of the 'Flight of Locks' (26) on the Kennet & Avon Canal at Devizes, now refurbished from dereliction by a preservation group; a tremendous task.

14. The approach to a 'Water Bridge' or aqueduct, with the actual 'bridge' portion in the background. Canal Engineering was required to continue the canal over a valley, or other stretch of water.

15. A rebuilt tramway truck for coal or stone. This example uses possibly original wheels and ironwork. Loose coupled to a horse, how effective the brake was raised an interesting question about the safety of the horse and the attendant should the truck run away! Overloading and rail breakage was always a problem with the cast-iron plate or edge rails, reduced slightly when the wrought-iron lengths were introduced, although, overloaded, they tended to bend. Shown are the 'fish belly' type. Each tramway had its own design and sizes of stone block sleeper.

16. All that remains of a Blenkinsop Rack rail tram engine. Ignoring, c. 1812, the example shown by Trevithick's Pennydarren tram road locomotive in c. 1804 of smooth rails and smooth wheels, designers were still very wary of the 'smooth' system. Note the rail design, chairs and stone 'sleepers'.

17. The Pennydarren Locomotive of Richard Trevithick – 1804.

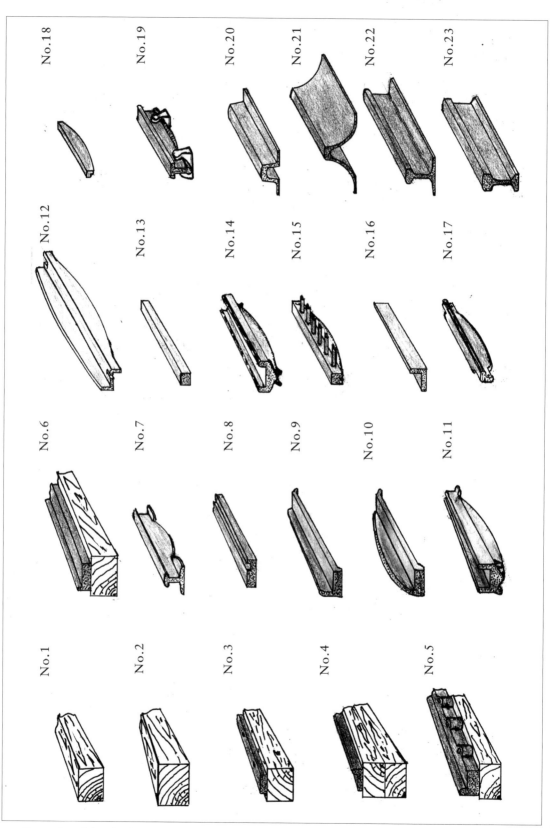

18. Examples of the development of the rail.

Ian Allan Bookshop
31 Royal Arcade
Cardiff
CF10 1AE
Tel No.02920 390615
FAX No.02920 340621
VAT No.GB 245 3027 42

£

at Western Railwa   5.00
rn Ticket   21.00

              No Items   2
         Including VAT   26.00
                                    26.00

                                 Id.   21
          14 Till:01 Audit:202744

          Gift Exchange
             anuary 201

Examples of the Development of the Rail Key to Illustrations

The Illustrations and list show rail designs associated with plateways and tramroads with continuous experimentation as the 'Railway' proper developed.

No.	Details
1	5-ft 4-in solid timber used in 1618 at Cowpen Colliery, Northumberland.
2	5-ft 6-in solid timber used 1733 at Prior Park (near Bath).
3	Wrought-iron strip set on a double timber base *c.* 1735.
4	Wrought-iron inside flange strip set on double timber, part bedded in the ground, *c.*1738 at Whitehaven, Cumberland.
5	Cast-iron inside flange strip with bolt lugs. Coalbrookdale Ironworks *c.* 1767. Cast by users.
6	Cast-iron outside flange rail. C1776. Duke of Norfolk's Colliery, Sheffield.
7	Cast-iron edge rail, part flat bottom, *c.* 1794, Jessop. Surprisingly 'modern'.
8	Cast-iron *c.* 1788, Nanpanton Colliery, Leicestershire. Flat cast iron with outside groove.
9	Cast-iron inside flange, *c.* 1799. Ben Outram's Ticknall 'Tramway'.
10	Cast-iron inside flange. Plymouth or Hill's Railway *c.* 1796.
11	Cast-iron channel flange, *c.* 1808. Wylam Colliery, Northumberland.
12	Cast-iron plate rail, *c.* 1803. Surrey Iron Railway.
13	Wrought-iron square section grooved wheel rail, *c.* 1806 at Walbottle and Tindale Fell.
14	Cast-iron channel flange 3-ft lengths, *c.* 1809, Silkstone.
15	Cast-iron Blenkinsop rack rail, *c.* 1812.
16	Cast-iron inside flange, *c.* 1814, Coalbrookdale.
17	Cast-iron Stephenson & Losh edge rail, 4-ft lengths. Also Swedish (*c.* 1816) malleable rails to same pattern 3 ft long. Fish-bellied design.
18	Cast-iron edge rail, 3-ft lengths, *c.* 1820, East Ardesley.
19	Wrought-iron edge rail, *c.* 1820. Cole Orton with a cast iron 'chair'.

Note:

From the mid-nineteenth century, a concerted effort was made with effective rail design. Numbers 20–23 show rail development from the mid-nineteenth century.

No.	Details
20	GWR BRIDGE RAIL – Used virtually for the duration of the broad gauge.
21	BARLOW RAIL – A special section tried during the 1850s but found wanting and replaced.
22	FLAT BOTTOM RAIL – In vogue for about forty years from 1846.
23	BULL HEAD RAIL – Various sections and weights per yard tried until about 1921 when BS9 was adopted for general use by the GWR. Long welded lengths later introduced. Current twenty-first-century decisions have made a return to flat bottom rail in very long lengths.

19. A preserved length of fish-bellied rail. Wrought-iron rail with scarfed joint ends.

20. Mixed (broad gauge and standard gauge) track at Didcot, with a disc and bar signal post. Gooch's Bridge Rail on Baulk Sleeper.

21. These three plates are from 'The Canal Viewer and Engine Builders' Practical Companion', published in 1797, and represent possibly the oldest technical drawings for construction of tramway rails and 'rolling stock', including cast-iron plate rails.

One of the earliest technical drawings for construction of a tramway 'Corf' (truck).

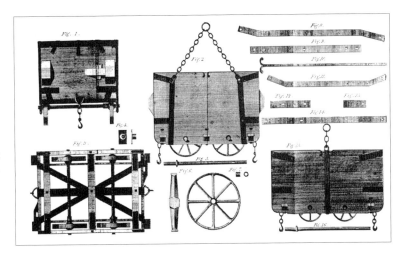

22. The new technical advance. Cast-iron tramway rails. Various straight, curves and crossover designs.

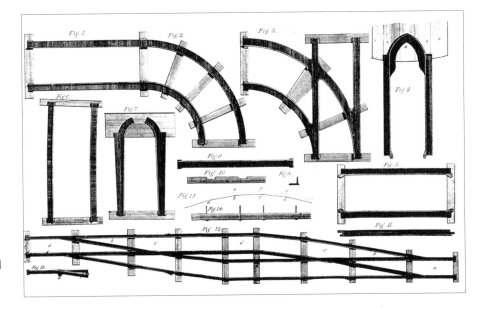

23. 'Corf' winding drum (Figs 5 & 10). Designs of 'Corves' with inside and outside wheels (Figs 3 & 8). Door-opening mechanism (Fig 9).

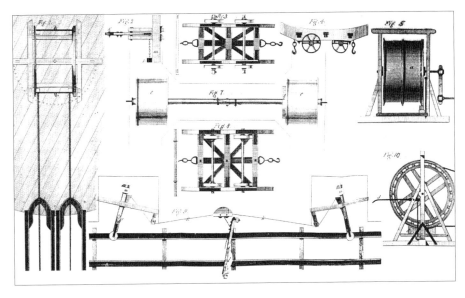

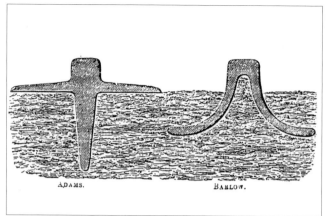 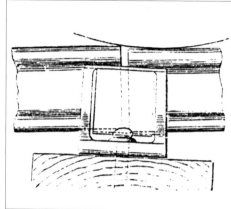

The following illustrations are from Clark's *Railway Machinery*.

Above left: 24. Comparative views of Barlow's saddle-back rail and girder rail proposed by W. B. Adams.

Above right: 25. The 'hammering' a rail joint received when a sleeper sank.

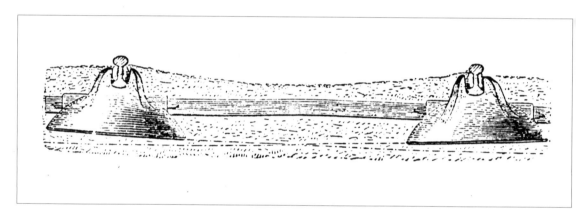

26. Greaves' surface-packed sleepers, with Douglas' fish-joint chairs.

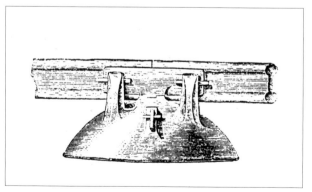 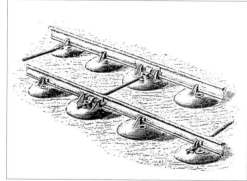

Above left: 27. Greaves' and Douglas' fish-joint chair and sleeper.

Above right: 28. Greaves' surface-packed sleepers.

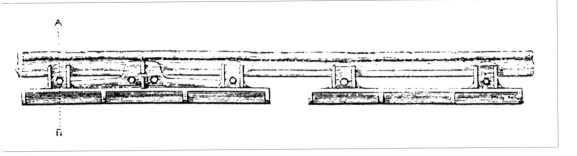

29. Mr P. W. Barlow's cast-iron sleepers.

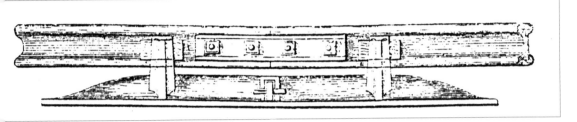

30. Mr W. H. Barlow's cast-iron fish-joint sleeper, as used on the Midland Railway.

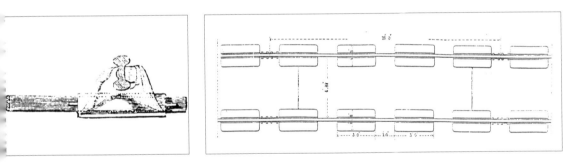

Above left: 31. Elevation.

Above right: 32. Samuel's cast-iron timber-bedded permanent way, with fish-joints.

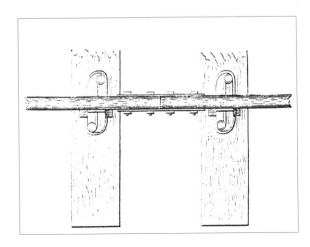

Right: 33. Fishing plates applied to ordinary rails.

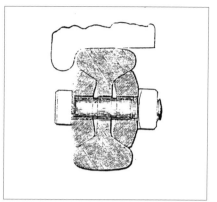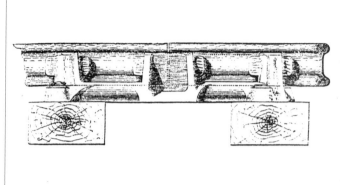

Above left: 34. Enlarged section of rail and fishing plates.

Above right: 35. Fowler's joint chair.

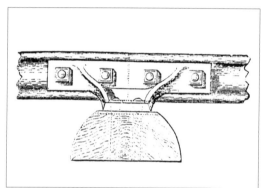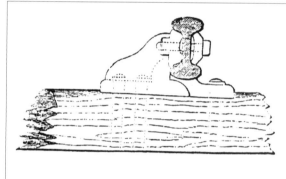

Above left, right and below: 36, 37 & 38. Samuel's fish chair.

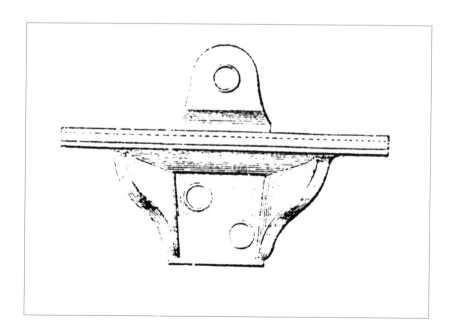

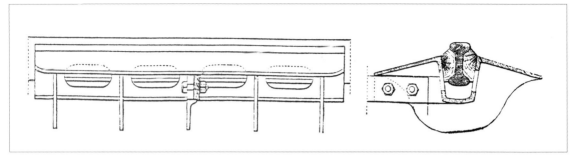

39. Detail of sleeper.

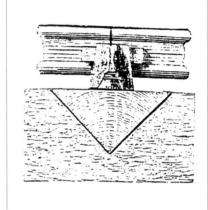

Above left: 40. Elevation of chair, showing the inclination of the rail.

Above right: 41. Joint chair – end view.

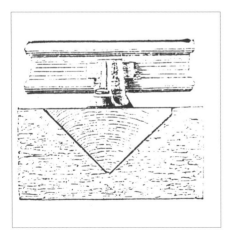

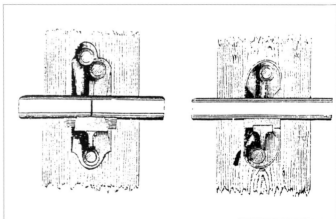

Above left: 42. Intermediate chair – end view.

Above right: 43. Plan.

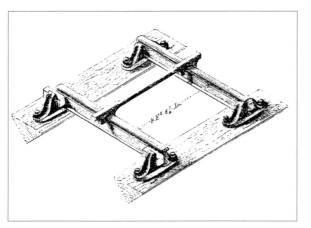

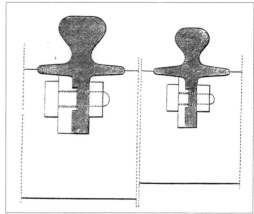

Above left: 44. Rails, chair and sleepers with the 'cramp-gauge' affixed. Ransomes & May's chairs and compressed wedges trenails.

Above right: 45. Girder rails by W. B. Adams.

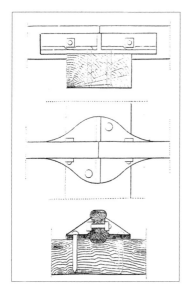

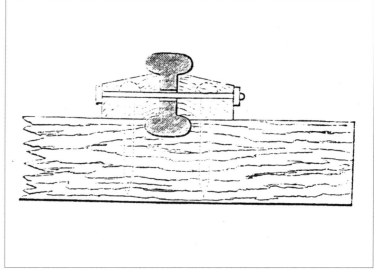

Above left: 46. W. B. Adams' cast-iron bracket-joint, without wood keys.

Above right: 47. Adam's rail without cast-iron chairs and with wood brackets.

Left: 48. W. H. Barlow's saddle-back rail, latest section.

49. 1750 Illustration of the tramway (gravity and manpower) at Prior Park, Bath (thought to be the earliest depiction of a tramway in Britain).

50. Linked horse power on a tramway.

51. 1822 – An early parallel Beam Colliery tramway locomotive with later 'cab' improvement.

52. A portion of the Rassa Tramroad photographed in 1913, still in use and open for 115 years at that time! Certainly not a high-speed route! 4-ft 2-in gauge steam tram engine from 1828.

53, 54 & 55. The 'Bedwelty' – A tramway locomotive from the Tredegar Coal & Iron Company. The top photograph shows the locomotive in its working days. The others show an abandoned and partially stripped item long out of use (tram engine from 1829). What a restoration project if it existed today! It was at the Tredegar Ironworks that Daniel Gooch started his career as a moulder.

56. An edge rail tramway truck of the Moreton & Stratford Tramway 1826. Preserved and photographed *c.* 1912 – having been abandoned in 1869. Note the fish bellied wrought-iron rail lengths on the stone sleeper blocks.

57. The last train on a standard gauge late tramway (1875). The Wantage to Wantage Road enterprise in Berkshire prior to closure in 1925.

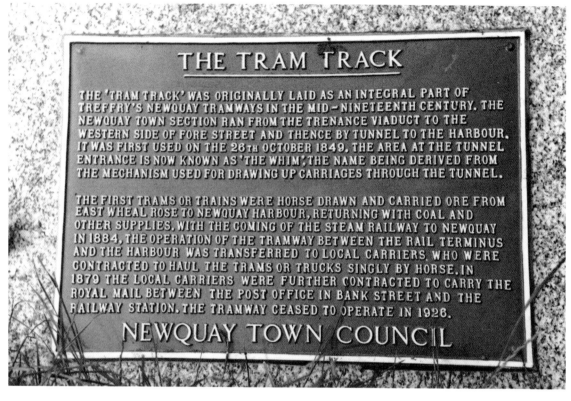

THE TRAM TRACK

THE 'TRAM TRACK' WAS ORIGINALLY LAID AS AN INTEGRAL PART OF TREFFRY'S NEWQUAY TRAMWAYS IN THE MID-NINETEENTH CENTURY. THE NEWQUAY TOWN SECTION RAN FROM THE TRENANCE VIADUCT TO THE WESTERN SIDE OF FORE STREET AND THENCE BY TUNNEL TO THE HARBOUR. IT WAS FIRST USED ON THE 26TH OCTOBER 1849. THE AREA AT THE TUNNEL ENTRANCE IS NOW KNOWN AS 'THE WHIM', THE NAME BEING DERIVED FROM THE MECHANISM USED FOR DRAWING UP CARRIAGES THROUGH THE TUNNEL.

THE FIRST TRAMS OR TRAINS WERE HORSE DRAWN AND CARRIED ORE FROM EAST WHEAL ROSE TO NEWQUAY HARBOUR, RETURNING WITH COAL AND OTHER SUPPLIES. WITH THE COMING OF THE STEAM RAILWAY TO NEWQUAY IN 1884, THE OPERATION OF THE TRAMWAY BETWEEN THE RAIL TERMINUS AND THE HARBOUR WAS TRANSFERRED TO LOCAL CARRIERS WHO WERE CONTRACTED TO HAUL THE TRAMS OR TRUCKS SINGLY BY HORSE. IN 1879 THE LOCAL CARRIERS WERE FURTHER CONTRACTED TO CARRY THE ROYAL MAIL BETWEEN THE POST OFFICE IN BANK STREET AND THE RAILWAY STATION. THE TRAMWAY CEASED TO OPERATE IN 1926.

NEWQUAY TOWN COUNCIL

58. Memorial to a mine tramway but really the broad story of them all.

59. Treffry's tramway bed and footbridge exists in the twenty-first century as a pedestrian walkway, a reminder of the original horse powered railways.

60. Example of plate rail and truck.

61. An example of a tramway truck on a very narrow edge rail. The narrow rails very quickly wore

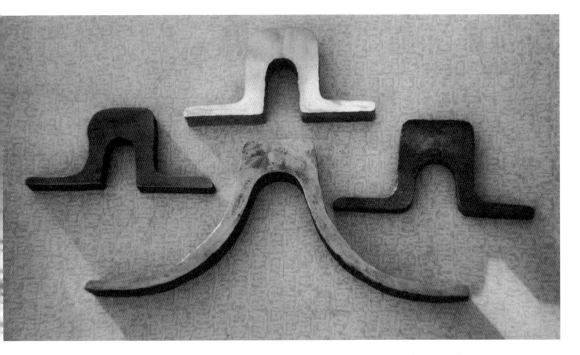

62. Sections of broad gauge rail: Three bridge type and Barlow rail. (Author's Collection)

63. A rather confusing preserved example of short section edge rail. Early flat bottom track.

64. A combined edge and plate rail (*c.* 1836) with a special design of cast-iron chair on stone blocks.

65. Plate rail and stone block sleepers with chairs.

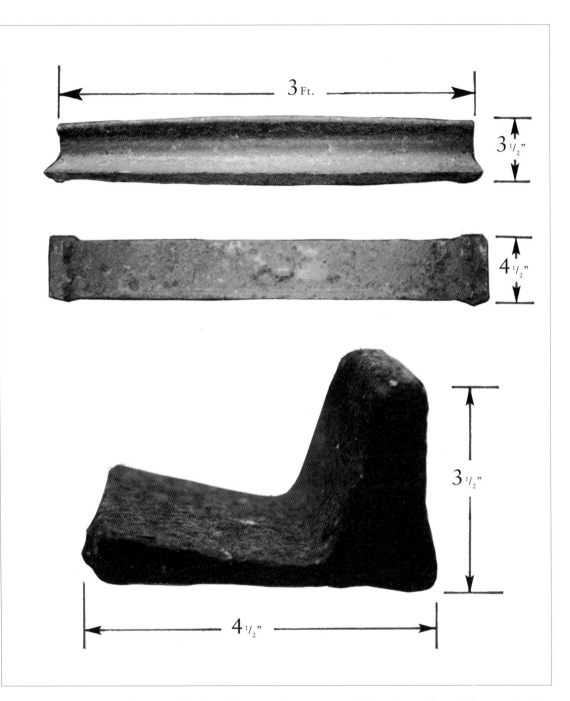

66. A tramway plate reputedly from the Pennydarren Tramroad, this plate rail could have carried the locomotive of Richard Trevithick, as the world's first steam railway. Weight: 49 lb. (Author's Collection)

Top: Side View – note convex top edge.
Middle: Underside of Base – note end locating lugs.
Bottom: An end view – wheels ran within inside angle.

Weight 98 lb.

67. The 'car gwyllt' – basically a seat on wheels – was used by the quarrymen to descend from Craig Ddu Quarry at the end of the working day. The car gwyllt was usually made by the quarrysmith for a few shillings and was light enough to be carried on the shoulders. Photographed by Geoff Charles in 1960, reproduced courtesy the National Library of Wales.

68. A convoy of cier gwylltion descends from Craig Ddu Quarry, c. 1900.

Bristol and Exeter Railway Company.

Debenture, No. 4790 £300.

GLYN

LONDON
8 10 69

By Virtue of an Act passed in the Sixth Year of the Reign of his late Majesty, King William the Fourth, intituled "*An Act for making a Railway from Bristol to Exeter, with Branches to the Towns of Bridgwater in the County of Somerset, and Tiverton in the County of Devon*," and of the several subsequent Acts relating to the Bristol and Exeter Railway Company, or some or one of them, WE, THE BRISTOL AND EXETER RAILWAY COMPANY, incorporated by and under the said first-mentioned Act, in Consideration of the Sum of *Three hundred* Pounds to us in hand paid by

Joan Ellis,

of 14 Regent Street, St Thomas the Apostle, Exeter, Widow,

Do assign unto the said *Joan Ellis,*

her Executors, Administrators, and Assigns, the said Undertaking and all and singular the Rates, Tolls, and Sums of Money arising by virtue of the said several Acts, and each and every and any of them, and all the Estate, Right, Title, and Interest of the said Company, in and to the same; **To hold** unto the said

Joan Ellis, her Three hundred

Pounds, together with Interest for the same after the Rate of *Four pounds five shillings* for every One Hundred Pounds for a Year, payable as hereinafter mentioned, shall be fully paid and satisfied. And it is hereby stipulated that the said Principal Sum of *Three hundred* Pounds shall be repayable and paid on presentation of this Debenture, duly receipted, at the Banking House of ~~Messrs. Glyn, Mills, Currie, and Company, London~~ *the National Provincial Bank of England, Bishopsgate* STREET, LONDON, on the FIFTH Day of *October* which will be in the Year One Thousand Eight Hundred and *seventy five*, from which day all liability for the payment of Interest shall cease, unless otherwise previously agreed between the Parties; and that in the meantime, the said Company shall, in respect of Interest as aforesaid on the said Principal Sum, pay to the bonâ fide Holder hereof, or to the Agents of such Holder, or to Persons duly authorized to receive the same, the several Sums mentioned in the Coupons or Interest Warrants hereto annexed, at the times specified therein. **Given** under the Common Seal of the said Company, this *seventh* day of *October* One Thousand Eight Hundred and *seventy.*

THE BRISTOL AND EXETER RAILWAY COMPANY.—*We, the Undersigned, being Two of the Directors of the Company, specially authorized and appointed for this purpose,—and I, the undersigned Registered Officer of the Company,—do hereby declare, each for himself, that the above-written Mortgage Deed is issued under the Borrowing Powers of the Company as registered on the* 11th *Day of* July 1870, *and is not in excess of the Amount there stated as remaining to be borrowed. Dated this* 7th *Day of* Oct. 1870.

Directors.

Secretary, and Registered Officer.

This and next page: 69 & 70. Bristol & Exeter Railway Share Certificate.

Received the amount of the within named Principal Sum of Three hundred Pounds (£300) with all interest due thereon :— Dated August 16th 1875

71. Original Bristol & Exeter Railway Offices, in use *c.* 1921 as Great Western Railway General Offices. An example of the elaborate classical buildings favoured by the developing early companies.

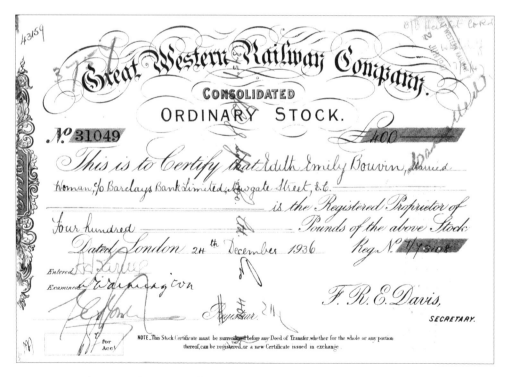

72. A GWR share certificate, cancelled on Nationalisation in 1947. The desire for investment remained until the end of the company itself, and shares continued to change hands as investors bought and sold on the market. This late investment example was to last only a decade.

London & North Western R⁷ & ᵈ Great Western Railway Companies

London Terminus.
Paddington. W.
20ᵗʰ March 1874

Robert Broughton Esq
Ruyton of the Eleven Towns
Salop

Sir.

The Directors having the management of the Railways vested jointly in the London & North Western and Great Western Railway Companies, having decided to replace the Debenture Bonds of such joint Railways, by the issue in equal moieties of the separate Debenture Stocks of the two Companies, we are instructed in respect of the Debenture Bond N° 464 for £550 of the Shrewsbury & Hereford Railway falling due on the 29ᵗʰ Proximo, to offer to convert the Bond from that date into £275 of London & North Western and £275 of Great Western 4 per Cent Debenture Stock at par nett, or the two Companies will repay the principal sum on its due date. —

Should you prefer repayment of the Loan on its maturity the money may be received by presenting the Debenture at the London Joint Stock Bank, N° 5 Princes Street, London, endorsed by yourself and M⁷ William Lloyd Asterley in the following form viz.ᵗ "Received the within mentioned

"principal sum of Five hundred and fifty pounds, together "with all Interest due thereon" and the Interest will cease from the date the loan falls due. —

Yours faithfully
Stephen Reay
Secretary per [signature]
London & North Western Railway Company

Fred: G. Saunders
Secretary per [signature]
Great Western Railway Company

P.S. Please address your reply as soon as possible to "The Secretary, Great Western Railway, Paddington. W.

73 & 74. Letter Referring to Stock in the LNWR and GW Railway.

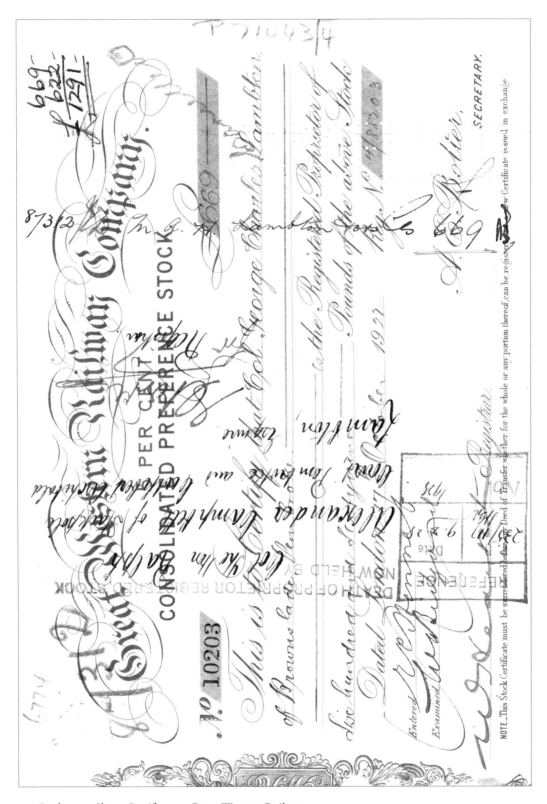

75. Preference Share Certificate – Great Western Railway.

76, 77, 78 & 79. Examples of four company seals.

80, 81 & 82. Seals of various absorbed companies.

83. The Canal Rebuilders

A phase of Great Western construction ended at Hay Lane Wharf, just outside Swindon, on the Wilts & Berks Canal. Now a green field area with a couple of houses and a garden centre, and known only to old Swindonians as 'Hay Lane Wharf', the road sign above is the only indication left of an association with a canal, slowly being reclaimed, but currently part of a green field, flat, the clay lining hidden beneath the filling.

84. A new bridge spans a cleared section of the Wilts & Berks Canal just outside Swindon, an example of canal activity across the country.

85. Taken from the new bridge, the author remembers this view as a complete green field, and the cleared section of the previous photograph as a reed choked, mud filled canal bed. There are currently (2010) detailed plans for an extension of the above section of the Wilts & Berks Canal into the heart of Swindon, taking a new route and bypassing the now grassed-over route of part of the original, which may be easily traced. Time will tell if such plans come to fruition.

86. Looking the other way. Railway bridge over the canal, showing canal reinstatement efforts (and of course the inevitable twenty-first-century graffiti).

3

The Great Western & Other Railway Companies

When mention is made of 'The Great Western Railway', the immediate concept which springs to mind is that of a massive organisation, its area spread like a giant triangular flag, its point in London and its base corners secured by the tip of Cornwall in the South and Birkenhead in the North.

We all seem to lose sight of the fact that, when proposed as the 'London & Bristol Railway', it was basically no different from the dozens of other railways proposed at the time. A transport concept in the midst of many others similarly conceived in all parts of the country, to join two important commercial cities by the shortest and best route; in this case to join London to Bristol, by the fast-developing 'Steam Railway', published along with other details. In company with other railway proposals, the shares were snapped up.

Even the business men, who, along with the other entrepreneurs elsewhere with the same ideas had decided to cash in on the new railways, were taken somewhat aback when their engineer, Brunel, insisted upon a very broad track gauge. The odd figure of 4 ft 8½ in was being bandied about freely among those of the railway fraternity, but already the 'think big' concept had been formed, and with Great Western, 7 ft was the figure to be used, with the later addition of a ¼-in to give more clearance.

With such a dynamic and persuasive man at the head of 'engineering' in its broadest sense, although he was not an actual 'locomotive' engineer as such, the sheer weight of ideas and far thinking laid the foundations of the company as we now know it, the popular concept of 'The Great Western'.

The year 1921 is always uppermost in railway minds as the year in which the four main railway groups were formed. From the number of smaller, nominally independent companies which were involved in running railways throughout the country, the establishing of the 'big four' was to be a simplification and 'standardisation' attempt, short of 'Nationalisation', which itself had been considered.

Under the Railway Act of 1921, four major new railway companies were formed, of which the only one to retain its old title was the Great Western Railway. This retention was greatly influenced by the differences of amalgamation of the various satellite companies into the parent company.

In the case of the Southern, the London, Midland & Scottish, and London North Eastern companies, the satellites, or at least some of the satellites, had been of approximately equal size and importance. In the case of the Great Western, it was the large company absorbing a number of very small companies, the only ones left after a century of expansion and development of the Great Western!

The amalgamation by the Great Western was to take about three years, beginning actually a year ahead of the specified date, and finishing early in 1924.

Many and varied were the locomotives taken over, nearly a thousand of them, all to varying styles and design, although few of the companies absorbed had possessed 'tender' type engines, most being of the 'tank' variety, either side or saddle tank or in a few cases a combination of both. Most were built by contractors, few of the companies having their own construction facilities.

Because of condition and differing maintenance standards, many of those absorbed were either scrapped or rebuilt, entailing in the latter case the use of as much Great Western standard material and components as possible. The standard green of the Great Western Railway, its number plate design, and in particular the chimney form and boiler with boiler mountings were all introduced as the locomotives were shopped for overhaul.

Some of the locomotives were comparatively new, and continued to give up to about thirty years of good service, but none of the classes absorbed were ever adopted as a 'Great Western' standard class, to have other new engines constructed to the same design, although some of the better locos of the same design formed an accepted class. In some cases the 'Great Westernising' included use of the tapered boiler design when renewals occurred, and led to very often strange looking hybrid types which the Great Western connoisseur viewed with some distaste, but which nevertheless added to the effectiveness of the locomotive, good looks being only skin (or lagging!) deep. Few of the absorbed locomotives had been built by their parent company, most constructed on contract by the many firms in the locomotive building business.

However, such talk of 'amalgamation' in 1921, the date which springs so readily to mind, is really jumping the gun. As stated at the beginning of this book, the amalgamations, leasings, takeovers, bankruptcies etc. of companies is not a modern phenomenon, it has occurred since the beginning of railways themselves, long before the steam locomotive, and into the days of the horse tramroads and plateways.

Within a very short time from its inception in 1836 the Great Western was on the track of its rivals, in more ways than the accepted meaning that the figure of speech implies. From the beginning of its running to its own demise on Nationalisation in 1948, the Great Western Railway absorbed, initiated, or took over, in one way or another, an astonishing number of other railway companies.

In some cases, several companies had already banded themselves together under a group name or under a 'parent' company, and it was the parent or group name company that the Great Western Railway eventually absorbed. It was like small boys playing 'conkers' with horse chestnuts! When you broke your opponents 'conker' you added not only that victory to your own score, but also the number of victories claimed by the owner of the 'conker' just broken. And 'broken' is the word for some of the companies taken over.

From such small beginnings, on a par with virtually everyone else at the time, most takeovers occurred before 1900, the final large takeover being the amalgamation of 1921, compulsorily placed on the Great Western and all other companies of the time throughout Britain. The Great Western had thus already eliminated, by merger, leasing and absorption, any company which had been or could be classed as 'opposition', in any sense of the word, years before 1921. As we have seen, the early 'opposition' included a number of established canals which were quite ruthlessly harassed to closure.

When the broad spaced rails of the Great Western were inexorably creeping toward Bristol, through the White Horse Vale, the visit of Brunel and Gooch in their quest for a rolling stock repair depot and stabling site indicated potential in other directions.

To the East, the equally unfinished track of the Cheltenham & Great Western Union Railway, its tracks scheduled to join up with the Great Western near Swindon, would give access to Cheltenham, in addition to the London–Bristol link. In the 'V' formed by the joint, would spring up the nucleus of the Swindon Railway Works.

The formation of a repair works so early in the life of a comparatively new company shows an astonishing confidence in the future. Whilst still only really an embryo of a railway – indeed its sole initial object of a line between London and Bristol was not yet finished – the location in the middle of nowhere for a maintenance depot sums up the Great Western. Think Big! It is even more astonishing to introduce the concept of actually *constructing* locomotives at the works at such an early stage in the railways development, a concept which followed rapidly on the works completion.

There were connections relevant to the Cheltenham & Gloucester Great Western Union Railway (C&GWU) that were far older than the line itself, and older than the Great Western, although the C&GWU and the Great Western were spawned in the same year, 1836. The connection absorbed into the C&GWU was that of the Cheltenham & Gloucester Plate Railway, which dated between Nelson's famous victory at Trafalgar and Napoleon's defeat at Waterloo, being incorporated in 1809. The potential of little trucks pulled by horses awaiting the arrival of a far more powerful type of a horse!

Also closely associated with the Great Western, the broad gauge Bristol & Exeter Railway started operations on the same day that the full Great Western line was opened, the complexities of routing the Great Western under the hills at Box having been overcome by tunnelling. By 1841, the Great Western had already started to expand, having opened in 1838 with just 22 miles of completed track.

As well as the importance of locomotive design and development, the first requirement of a railway is that it has to actually go somewhere, joining places of commercial importance as envisaged at the time. Many entrepreneurs of the period were quite aware of this premise, and the proposals were pushed with great enthusiasm to join all sorts of main towns and cities in portions of the country in which the Great Western showed more than a passing interest.

It must be remembered that at this period also, a number of the other companies that blossomed were on a par in size, status, and financial backing, with the Great Western itself. Whether this would include the same ruthlessness is a matter of opinion, but certainly the forcefulness of the Board often governed the success of the enterprise.

Parliamentary records of the nineteenth century are littered with proposals and counter-proposals for railway bills promoted and opposed by the contenders in this enterprise free-for-all. Included in this chapter, in alphabetical order with takeover date or order of Great Western 'takeover', is a list of the companies which, in one way or another, became enmeshed in the Great Western expansion net, and remember there are over 230 of them! Some are only very small, just a few miles in extent, and usually using leased rolling stock, but nevertheless, separate companies, several of which were associated with docks and canals. Some had already combined together under a different name, before takeover. Some were never built although authorised! Some had developed from tramroads and plateways.

It was often the case that the Great Western 'allowed' a company to fight its local opposition by itself, whether canal or other railway. When successfully concluded, and the company had expanded or won some other financial or material battle, in stepped the Great Western with a takeover proposal. A case in point is that of the Bristol & Exeter, which fought the Grand Western Canal to a standstill, as outlined in Chapter One, and then became part of the Great Western.

In these 'battles of the nineteenth century', the Great Western, by its record very successful in these matters, didn't always get everything its own way. Continual opposition in the early years was experienced from both the London North Western Railway and from, coincidentally, the London South Western Railway, to name but two sources. In all these battles, the broad gauge was usually the stumbling block.

Captain Huish, chairman of the board of the London North Western Railway, appeared to have a pathological hatred of the Great Western and everything connected with it.

It must also be said that the captain had a hatred of everything and everybody associated in any way with any form of opposition to him and 'his' railway. As with his attitude to the Great Western, so it was with Edmund Denison's Great Northern, fighting to extricate itself from the tangled web of intrigue and violence spun by Captain Huish and his 'confederacy' of companies. To be viable, a railway has to go somewhere and join major nuclei of commerce or industry, and the Great Northern was bedevilled by Huish's machinations for many years. Whilst really outside the scope of this book, indeed it could form a book by itself, the story of blocked lines, trapped locomotives, denial of legal running powers, thugs with one specially given free share attending, and breaking up, shareholders' meetings held by companies interested in joining the Great Northern, make interesting reading. As a guide to some Victorian business methods it is also quite frightening. Denison beat him in the end, and Huish was disgraced in a way similar to the previous railway 'king', George Hudson, both of whom had gone beyond business bounds in the search for power.

Starting in the early years of the narrow versus broad gauge controversy, an anti-broad gauge publicity drive was initiated by the LNWR in an attempt to strangle the Great Western, by trying endlessly to stop the spread of the broad gauge. Purchase by the Great Western in 1846 of two 'narrow' gauge lines, the Birmingham & Oxford Railway and the Birmingham, Wolverhampton & Dudley Railway, with permission to extend the spread of broad gauge to Birmingham via the two lines concerned, was probably the last Northern expansion success for the broad track.

A few years later, the acquisition of the Shrewsbury & Birmingham and the Shrewsbury & Chester Railways – both narrow gauge – included in the amalgamation Act of 1854 strict clauses which prohibited the extension of broad gauge above Wolverhampton. A line initiated by the Great Western, the Oxford, Worcester & Wolverhampton (OW&W) Railway actually rebelled in 1851 in favour of narrow gauge. Irrespective of Parliamentary Acts and various paper 'agreements', the OW&W Railway had to be forced to lay broad gauge rails.

It was still showing great determination to defy the Great Western and remain narrow! This it did by the subterfuge of laying joint broad and narrow gauge tracks, and then only using the narrow version. Who, in retrospect, is to say they were wrong? By this means the narrow lines eventually penetrated the heart of the Great Western Mecca at Paddington! Lines of what could be classed as the 'National' gauge.

To the South, signatures on documents foretold that broad gauge would reach such points as Basingstoke, Salisbury, Yeovil, Hungerford and to the sea at Weymouth, but too many disputes and too little cash meant a stalemate in actual lines completed, so little was done. Attempts into Dorset and Devon met the same fate, where the question of National Defence raised its head. In the height of a transport crisis occasioned by a war, it was obviously not a bit of use to have to switch loads from one set of trucks to another just because the widths between rail tracks could not be made uniform! The tracks in the defence areas were already to the narrow gauge.

By the mid-1850s the broad gauge Great Western was no longer solely broad gauge! Fighting all the way, but losing many of the important battles, the front to the North of Wolverhampton had been consolidated as narrow gauge, 80 miles of it, which had to remain so! It is true that broad gauge was still being laid in the 1860s, but only very short lengths of branches and odd additional lengths extending existing tracks.

On 1 June 1877, a short branch from St Erth, previously called St Ives Road, was laid into St Ives. This short track proved to be the last broad gauge ever laid as new.

It may come as something of a surprise to the reader, but not only were dual broad and narrow lines laid in the well known 'mixed gauge' format to enable either 'broad' or 'narrow' gauge trains to use the same route, but mixed gauge *trains* were also run in several places. In 1871, the very strange sight of a narrow gauge engine with narrow gauge trucks followed by broad gauge trucks could be seen between Truro and Penzance.

This was certainly a complicated way of using up existing stock! The joint between narrow and broad trucks was made by inserting a specially adapted 'match truck' on the broad gauge. With special sliding couplings and special 'buffers', it allowed the joint to be made between trucks of different widths in which wheels of one side on every truck ran on the same rail, wheels on the other side running on the 'narrow' rail and 'broad' rail respectively. The wagons were not, of course, symmetrically placed, the narrow gauge pulling the broad gauge trucks 'off centre'.

Great care had to be exercised in negotiating points and crossings, as the narrow gauge portion had to do a double shuffle sideways either to right or left, a move undertaken at the slowest speed possible! This double track use was not confined to goods traffic. Moving from West Cornwall to the 'Royal' branch at Windsor, we find mixed gauge passenger trains running under the same arrangements, joined by a special truck between broad and narrow portions.

Broad gauge was still in evidence, but trains were reducing on the broad and increasing on the narrow and mixed tracks. Conversions to narrow gauge were being undertaken all over the remaining broad gauge system, the stock of the latter being reduced, but there were certain areas where broad would be retained as long as possible.

After problems with the London North Western (LNW), the London South Western (LSW) were, and had been, a thorn in the paw of the Great Western over a number of years, and the fear was that if too many narrow conversions were made, the L&SW Railway would demand running powers over the narrow track and thus be the thin end of the wedge into Great Western preserves! To continue the narrow gauge along the 'military' South Coast, the L&SW immediately offered their services, but had to be 'leaned on' by the government, after a three-year delay of doing nothing, to fulfil their pledge. The broad gauge meanwhile continued to diminish.

The Bristol & Birmingham (B&B) Railway, which included a refurbished early tram road, was very sympathetic to Great Western overtures to takeover, but haggling over share offer prices delayed the acquisition. A minute, in share terms, increase in the offer would have secured the company for the Great Western, but stubbornness on the part of the Great

Western with regard to an increase allowed the thrusting Midland Railway to snatch the prize from right under the noses of the Great Western Board, taking over in 1845.

The snatching of the newly formed B&B Railway was summed up very clearly by the Deputy Chairman of the Midland (who had seized the opportunity virtually out of thin air and without the knowledge of his board). His explanation of his actions, triggered by an almost chance meeting with representatives of the B&B, themselves *en route* to a meeting with Great Western representatives, included the statement 'When offered to me ... better to run the risk of losing a few thousand pounds than admit the plague of the broad gauge to Birmingham ...' One of the constituent companies of the B&B had been the broad gauge Bristol & Gloucester (the other was the Birmingham & Gloucester), which the Midland continued to run, but by 1854, the narrow gauge had arrived and the broad gauge stock was sold to the Bristol & Exeter Railway. Apart from one stubbornly defended broad gauge coal train which ran over a short section of the line on a daily trip from Parkfield Colliery until 1826, the broad gauge lines remained *in situ* and rusting until 1872, never used again by the Great Western.

The old B&G further complicated matters by having a running agreement with the Avon & Gloucester Railway, which was to 4-ft 8-in gauge, the old tramway mentioned earlier. 4-ft 8-in tracks were laid inside 7 ft of the broad gauge, the old fish bellied rails used for the purpose, removed from stone blocks of the original setting, and re-laid on iron sleepers set between the longitudinal sleepers of the 7 ft! This was thus the first example of 'mixed gauge' ever laid, and although as early as 1839, indicated the future problems which would bedevil the expanding rail networks. It was also proposed that the tramway continue using horses, soon found to be impracticable.

With the loss of the B&B Railway, the threat of broad gauge to the soil of the Midlands had been removed, and became probably the greatest defeat suffered by the expanding Great Western Railway (GWR). The GWR and the Midland were still at daggers drawn and fighting legal battles well into the twentieth century. A dispute settled by a court ruling in 1908 was the culmination of routing arguments, the Great Western still smarting and suffering from its defeat of sixty years before during the shares offer fight. The loss of the Bristol to Birmingham route was still sorely felt.

Underestimating the costs of a project, so much a seemingly modern phenomenon, was a problem to many new companies from the very beginnings of railways. In the early years, plans to open up large stretches of countryside to the benefits of rail travel were submitted for approval by a number of opposing companies, each sure it had the best route mapped out. The opposition to the London and Birmingham route, in the form of the Oxford, Worcester & Wolverhampton (OW&W), was costed and supported by no less a person than Brunel, in the hope of spreading his beloved broad gauge rails right into the Midlands. Again he was frustrated, and his estimate of costs was a far cry from the actual amount, being two and a half times the original £1 million, a tremendous variation in the 1840s, being bad enough in modern times. This was not the only time he badly underestimated – his South Devon Atmospheric venture is another prime example.

Whilst the battles for new route sanctions were being waged through and around Parliament, equally fierce fights were continually waged for the right of 'running powers' over the tracks of other companies. To get from point A to B may have been a desirable achievement, but often it meant that a portion of the route was already covered by someone else's railway! Therefore, to make a 'through' connection, permission had to be obtained to allow running over this section. If the companies involved did not see eye-to-eye in any case over some other real or imagined grievance, this could prove very difficult to arrange. Among a number of incidents which occurred under these circumstances, the two following will indicate the nature of the problem and the results of such antagonism.

The LNW Railway had by mid-century completed, but was seemingly reluctant to open, the Stour Valley Railway line from Birmingham to just beyond Wolverhampton to a connection with the Grand Junction tracks. Pressures were applied from various sources for an opening, and as soon as likely dates emerged the Shrewsbury & Birmingham (S&B) Railway jumped in to apply their running powers agreements over the tracks. A haggle followed, in which the LNW Railway claimed that, as the S&B Railway had merged with the GWR (which at that stage, 1851, it hadn't, although proposed to do so some time in the future!), running powers no longer existed! This was a red rag to the S&B bull, which announced that it *would* run over the line, and issued a timetable with time and date to show it meant business!

When the first S&B train arrived, it was confronted by the LNW Railway locomotive *Swift* (back up by another loco and its tender, thus blocking both Up and Down tracks), and a crowd of LNW Railway supporters. Coming from the opposite direction the S&B train slowly advanced hissing steam from the safety valve and whistle open, through red flags and fog signals to push its buffers tight against the firmly brake-locked *Swift*. With the local militia on standby, and the crowds of police everywhere, the contestants cooled down somewhat after summonses were obtained against various members of the obstructing group, including the engine driver. The 'through route' was postponed for a month, and when reluctantly forced to open up again, the LNW Railway arranged its timetables so that nothing connected with anything run by the S&B! Arguments still raged over any trivial items the LNW Railway could think of, ranging from tolls to engine inspections, the latter for 'safety and suitability', and the dispute continued for upward of two years more.

It must not be assumed that the Great Western was the 'blue-eyed boy' during this period, and it was not averse to using such strong arm tactics itself, when it considered the occasion demanded! It was thought to be such an occasion when the tentacles of the Midland Railway were seen to be wriggling too far into what were considered by the GWR to be its preserves in the area of Hereford.

A contest had evolved in the Mid Wales area between several companies, each with its eye on Brecon, various ideas eventually becoming the Hereford, Hay & Brecon (HH&B) Railway, incorporated in 1859. Around this period, with progressive advances up the Wye Valley by the contractor working the railway, a merger with the Brecon & Merthyr was given the thumbs down by authority and declared illegal! The Midland Railway, always on the lookout for a sneaky way into South Wales, made a strong bid for the HH&B Railway increasing its grip by first running goods traffic through Worcester to Hereford, and then passengers during 1869.

The Great Western decided enough was enough and proceeded to chop off a Midland tentacle or two! Goods traffic was bad enough but passengers – never! Thus the Midland passenger train which approached Hereford's Barton Station during that day in 1869 would have been announced as 'The train approaching Platform One will be completely blocked by a locomotive with its brakes screwed down, and by a line of wagons – so there!' When the usual fist-waving opponents had departed, along with the head-to-head locomotive encounter, and the dust had settled, the Midland had taken the hint that they were not welcome.

Although increasing their grip on the HH&B Railway, which they eventually absorbed in 1876, they retreated to Moorfields Station which they continued to use for a number of years, the lesson of the Barton blockade well and truly learned. Main line passenger traffic was not attempted again, although a successful goods service developed. Becoming a victim of the cuts of the 1960s, part of the HH&B Railway survives in a length used by the Bulmers Railway Centre, preservers in later years of the Great Western's *King George V*, noted itself for blocking a track when it had a hot box on an enthusiast's run! A far cry from the blockades of a century before, now residing in the National Railway Museum, York.

The break of gauge (7¼ ft / 4 ft 8½ in) problem was continually to the fore wherever boundary crossings onto someone else's railway was required, and various methods were proposed, and rejected, for speeding up transfers of goods. Passengers could walk, with a little inconvenience from one train to another, but literally mountains of parcels and packages, animals and bulk loads, the internal commerce of a nation, was a different matter. Trucks with sliding wheels on broad gauge axles, broad gauge trucks carrying narrow gauge trucks, even a 'container' system were all proposed and all were rejected. The conclusion which was inevitably arrived at by everyone except the Great Western was that of unified 4 ft 8½ in!

The mixing of tracks on the existing and future railways of the country was also subjected to arguments, proposals and counter-proposals. The many small new railways which had emerged in all sorts of places had been subjected to pressures from all sorts of sources on the benefits, or otherwise, of the two main track widths. Depending on initiators or supporters for these railways was the direction which arguments would take in supporting or opposing the bills to be submitted through Parliament for such lines. Brunel clashed severely with Stephenson over the manner of application of 'mixed' gauge to the Oxford & Rugby Railway. Although Parliament and the Board of Trade had specified 'mixed track', it left to the company the best method thought to be for applying such instructions. Stephenson, a bitter opponent of both broad and 'mixed' track, became involved and was soundly slated by Brunel as being a known hostile participant who should not have been consulted in the first place! Someone with a broader unbiased view should have been involved.

In spite of these arguments and antagonisms, which lasted over the rest of the century, the Great Western continued an inexorable programme of takeover, absorptions, initiations, amalgamations, its boundaries and interests continually enlarging. It would take a series of volumes alone to chart the detail of the inclusion of every company taken into the fold of the GWR, a task well outside the scope of this book. A list of companies absorbed, by whatever means, by the GWR, now follows, and includes those companies absorbed in the final rationalisation of 1921–23. The companies absorbed prior to this period (the companies are listed in alphabetical order), show the very varied spread of the railway concept throughout the area embraced by what finally became 'The Great Western Railway', a far cry from a broad gauge line joining Bristol to London.

As mentioned previously, some companies had already been absorbed by other companies, and it was sometimes the combined group with its own new title which was absorbed by the Great Western, indirectly embracing all.

Great Western Development and Growth – Constituent Companies

The following two lists (and map, dated 1926), continue to record the story of the development and growth of the Great Western Railway (GWR).

The first list comprises the company names during the formative years of the Great Western. Over these years, the constituent companies had among themselves been subjected to takeovers, name changes, integrations, amalgamations, bankruptcies, proposals for new companies which came to nothing, and the initiation, often by the Great Western itself, of new companies or branches. On this list the companies are in alphabetical order. The first list is cross-referenced to the second list which is itself associated with the sectional Map. This map shows the position of the relevant company names indicated in numerical order on the second list. These names are often the final names of companies which themselves incorporated other smaller companies before succumbing to takeover by the Great Western.

All culminated in 1921–23 with the formation of the 'Big Four'. The Great Western now controlled an even bigger area, which was to remain for twenty or so years, including the Second World War, until the dead hand of Nationalisation ended the official Great Western Railway story in 1947. With Nationalisation, the days of one company, one board, one chairman 'carrying the can' were lost in the mishmash of policies which appeared to elbow out the old independent Great Western. 'Privatisation' again reared its head when, instead of returning to the 'Big Four' (one company, one board, one chairman each), the Government reintroduced the fragmentation which the Great Western had spent 100 years eliminating. Now no one seems to control anything, and one company blames another if anything goes wrong (which appears to do with frightening regularity)! Where is there, in this twenty-first century, a modern-day Brunel and Gooch to start the consolidation process all over again?

List One (Alphabetical Listing)
Railway Companies Within the Areas of Influence of the GWR

Listing the GWR and its constituent and associated companies, and dates of absorption, purchase, takeover or initiation by GWR. Includes some not built, or lost to other than GWR.

No.	Map No.	Company Name	Ref to Tramroad	Year to GWR
1	56	Abbotsbury Railway. 1885. Closed 1952.		1896
2	187	Abercarn (see also Halls' Tramroad).	22	
3	202	Aberdare Railway Co. 1845. Leased to Taff Vale 1847. Absorbed 1902.		1922
4	227	Aberdare Valley Railway Co. 1857. Leased to Vale of Neath Railway then VN Railway. 1864.		1865
5	164	Aberystwyth & Welsh Coast Railway Co. 1861. Leased to Cambrian Railway 1865 (86 miles).		1922
6	88	Abingdon Railway Co. 1855.		1904

7	10	Acton & Wycombe Railway. 1897. GW & LNE and GC joint.		1899
8	99	Alcester Railway Co. 1872. Closed 1951 (6½ miles).		1878
9	58	Admiralty Line (see Portland Breakwater Railway).		
10	189	Alexandra Docks & Railway Co. 1865. Line absorbed Pontypridd, Caerphilly & Newport from 1897.		1922
11		Andoversford & Stratford-Upon-Avon Railway. 1898.		1899
12	93	Ashendon & Aynho Railway (GWR). 1905. Opened 1910.		1905
13		Aston & Brenford Railway Co. 1865.		
14		Avon & Gloucestershire Railway. 1828. Owned by Kennet & Avon Canal Co.	38	To Midland 1852
15	25	Avonmouth & Filton Railway (GWR). 1904. Opened 1910.		1904
16		Avonmouth Light Railway. 1908. Purchased by GWR and LMS.		1927
17	24	Avonmouth & Severn Tunnel Junction Railway (GWR). 1890. Opened 1900.		1890
18		Aylesbury & Buckingham Railway.		1867
19	109	Bala & Colgelly Railway Co. 1862. Worked by GWR from opening.		1877
20	110	Bala & Festiniog Railway Co. 1873. Worked by GWR from 1879.		1910
21	125	Banbury & Cheltenham Direct Railway Co. 1873. Purchased and line worked by GWR from 1886.		1897
22		Bangor & Caernarvon Railway.		
23	212	Barry Railway Co. 1884. Ex-Barry Dock & Railway Co.		1922
24	39	Berks & Hants Extension Railway Co. 1859. Worked by GWR from 1861.	1882	
25	38	Berks & Hants Railway Co. 1845. GWR-owned extension (31 miles).		1845
26	118 119	Birkenhead Railway. 1860. Taken over jointly with L&NW Railway. 1861.	1861	
27	120	Birkenhead, Lancashire & Cheshire Junction Railway. 1846. Name changed 1859.		
28		Bideford, Westward Ho & Appledore Railway. 1910/1908. Light railway with three 2-4-0 tank locos. Closed when government commandeered the track in 1917 for use in France.		
29	3	Birmingham, Bristol & Thames Junction Railway (see West London Railway).		
30	97	Birmingham & Henley-in-Arden Railway Co. 1873. Worked by GWR from 1888. Line closed and taken up 1917.		1900
31	98	Birmingham, North Warwickshire & Stratford-Upon-Avon Railway Co. 1984.		1907

32	95	Birmingham & Oxford Junction Railway Co. 1846. Originally narrow gauge.		1848
33	100	Birmingham, Wolverhampton & Dudley Railway Co. 1846. Originally narrow gauge.		1846
34		Bishops Castle Railway. 1861. A private line offered to the GWR who showed no interest.		
35		Bodmin & Cornwall Junction Railway. 1864. Not built.		Not built
36	124	Bourton-on-the-Water Railway Co. 1860. Opened 1862. (Kingham to Bourton 6½ miles).		1874
37		Bodmin & Wadebridge. 1834. (Illegally owned by L&SW Railway in 1847). Two locos and forty wagons.		
38		Bodmin, Wadebridge & Delabole. 1873. Abandoned and wound up 1878.		
39	76	Bodmin Railway Co. 1882. (GWR) Opened 1887.		1882
40		Brecon Junction Railway Co. Scheme abandoned.		
41	192	Brecon & Merthyr Tydfil Junction Railway Co. 1859.		1922
42		Bridgewater & Taunton Railway. Canal and Harbour. Failure to construct.		
43		Bridgewater Navigation & Railway. 1845. Taken over by B&E Railway 1859.		1876
44	55	Bridport Railway Co. 1857. Broad gauge until 1871. Extended 1884.		1901
45	133	Bridgnorth & Wolverhampton Railway. 1905. (GWR)		1905
46	27	Bristol & Exeter Railway Co. 1836. Absorbed Chard & Taunton (28), Cheddar Valley & Yatton (29), Exe Valley (30). Worked Nos 31, 32, 33 & 34.		1876
47		Bristol & Gloucestershire Railway. 1828. 10 miles 4-ft 8-in gauge, later broad gauge. Long negotiations with GWR failed, c. 1845.	37	To Midland Railway c. 1845
48	20	Bristol Harbour Railway. 1866. (Joint GWR, Bristol & Exeter Rly & Bristol Corporation)		1866
49	21	Bristol Harbour Extension Railway. 1897. (Joint GWR, Bristol & Exeter Rly & Bristol Corporation)		
50	51	Bristol & North Somerset Railway Co. 1863. Worked by GWR from 1867 (15 miles).		1884
51	31	Bristol & Portishead Pier Railway. 1867. To Bristol & Exeter Railway.		1876
52	23	Bristol Port Railway & Pier Co. 1846. Joint with Midland Railway.		1890
53		Bristol & S. Wales Junction. Replaced by Bristol & S Wales Union Railway. 1846.		1869
54	22	Bristol & S. Wales Union Railway Co. 1857. Worked by GWR from 1864.		1868
55	225	Briton Ferry Floating Dock Co. 1851. Purchased.		1873

56	239	Burry Port & Gwendraeth Valley Railway Co. 1866. Over Kidwelly & Llanelly Canal route.	136, 137, 138	1922
57	195	Bute Docks Co. 1886. Absorbed by Cardiff Railway 1897.		1922
58	60	Buckfastleigh, Totnes & S. Devon Railway Co. 1864. South Devon Railway 1873. Included ¾ mile of horse tramway (until 1874) from Totnes to quay on the Dart.		1897
59	188	Brymaur & Western Valleys Railway. Joint with London North Western 1902.		1906
60	19	Calne Railway Co. 1869.		1892
61	160/165	Cambrian Railway Co. (Oswestry & Westown, Lhanidloes & Newtown, Newtown & Machynlleth, Aberystwyth & West Coast). 1864/65.		1992
62	241	Carmathen & Cardigan Railway Co. Last broad gauge trains in Wales. Absorbed 1881. Purchased.	131, 132	1890
63	50	Camerton & Limpley Stoke Railway. 1904. Built on bed of Somerset Coal Canal Co. Purchased by GWR in 1903.		1904
64	220	Cardiff & Ogmore Valley Railway. 1873.		1873
65	209	Cardiff, Penarth & Barry Junction Railway Co. 1885. To Taff Vale 1889.		1923
66	195	Cardiff Railway Co. 1886.		1922
67	53	Castle Cary & Langport Railway. 1898.		1898
68		Cefn & Pyle Railway. 1876. Purchased by Port Talbot Railway 1897.		1922/08
69		Chard Railway Co. 1846. To London South Western 1863.		
70	28	Chard & Taunton Railway Co. 1861. Dissolved 1863. Taken over by Bristol & Exeter Railway.		1876
71		Chard Canal & Railway. 1846. Not built became Chard & Taunton Railway Co.		1876
72	29	Cheddar Valley & Yatton Railway. 1869–70. To Bristol & Exeter 1871.		1874
73	141	Cheltenham & Great Western Union Railway Co. 1836. Leased to GWR 1841. Absorbed by GWR 1843.		1843
74		Cheltenham & Oxford Railway Co. 1847. Part built only during 1862, 1866, 1881.		
75	143	Cheltenham & Honeybourne Railway. 1899.		1899
76	118	Chester & Birkenhead Railway. 1837. Joined with Birkenhead, Lancs & Cheshire Junction Railway to form Birkenhead Railway 1847.		(1861)
77	246	Clarbeston Road & Letterston Railway. 1898. (GWR)		1898
78	136	Cleobury, Mortimer & Ditton Priors Light Railway Co.		1922
79		Clifton Extension Railway & Port Railway. Joint FW & Midland. (Clifton Extension joint 1974).		1890

80		Clifton Rocks Railway. c. 1892. Private company. Closed 1934.		
81	149	Coleford, Monmouth, Usk & Pontypool Railway Co. 1853 (17 miles) Leased to GWR.		1861
82	151	Coleford Railway Co. 1872. Small portion of the Coleford, Monmouth, Usk & Pontypool Railway (not built).	40	1883
83	73	Cornwall Railway. 1846. Leased to GWR, Bristol, Exeter & South Devon 1859.		1889
84	77	Cornwall Minerals Railway Co. 1873. Absorbed and closed Par Canal 1873. 46¾ miles. Worked from 1877 and purchased by GWR in 1896.	66	1896
85		Corris Railway Co. 1864. Changed name from Corris, Machyntleth & River Dovey Tramroad 1858.		1930
86		Cork & Fermoy Railway Co. Defunct. Not completed.		
87	108	Corwen & Bala Railway Co. 1862. Worked by GWR from 1866.		
88		Cosford Camp & Sutton Veny Camp Railway. (Military lines built during First WW, taken over by GWR in 1918).		1918
89	208	Cowbridge & Aberthaw Railway. 1889. To Taff Vale Railway 1895.		1922
90	207	Cowbridge Railway Co. 1862. 5¾ miles. Leased by Taff. Vale Railway for 999 years 1876 and incorporated in 1889.		1922
91	36	Culm Valley Light Railway Co. 1873. Worked by Bristol & Exeter Railway. Purchased by GWR.		1880
92	235	Clydach Vale Colliery Railway. Private line. Purchased by Taff Vale 1899.		1992
93		Clydach, Pontardawe & Cwmgorse Railway. GWR 1911. To Colliery and Works.		1911
		Cwmfrwyd Railway and Tramroad (1792). From 1845. Remained independent.		
94	203	Dare Valley Railway Co. 1863. Promoted by Taff Vale Railway and incorporated 1889.		1922
95	67	Dartmouth & Torbay Railway Co. 1857. South Devon Railway 1864.		1876
96	113	Denbighshire Railway. 1896. (GWR)		1896
97		Devon & Cornwall Central Railway. 1882. To Plymouth, Devonport & SW Junction Railway 1883.		
98		Devon & Cornwall Railway. 1865. Late Okehampton Railway 1862.		To LSW Railway 1889
99		Devon & Dorset Railway. 1852. Proposal only by GWR. Not built.		Not built
100	32	Devon & Somerset Railway Co. 1864. 42¾ miles. Bristol & Exeter Railway 1873.		1876/1901
101	41	Didcot, Newbury & Southampton Railway Co. 1873. Worked by GWR 1882.		1923

102		Drayton Junction Railway Co. 1864. Abandoned not completed.		
103	216	Duffryn, Llynvi & Porthcawl. 1825. 17 miles. Joined Ogmore Valley Railway 1865. Absorbed by the Cardiff & Ogmore 1876.	116	1883
104	231	Dulas Valley Mineral Railway Co. 1862. Became the Neath & Brecon Railway 1963.		1922
105	59	Easton & Church Hope Railway. 1867. Joint with Southern.		1897
106	91	East Gloucestershire Railway Co. 1864.		1890
107	52	East Somerset Railway Co. 1856. 9 miles long.		1874
108	183	East Usk Railway Co. 1885. Taken over by GWR by Act of 28 July 1892.		1892
109	6	Ealing & Shepherds Bush Railway. 1905. GWR		1905
110	215	Ely & Clydach Valley Railway Co. 1873.		1880
111	214	Ely Valley Railway Co. 7½ miles. For Cilely Colliery coal for GWR engines. Leased by GWR 1880.		1903
112	218	Ely Valley Extension Railway. 1863. (2½ miles) Worked by GWR (see Ogmore Railway No. 219).		1863
113		Exeter & Crediton Railway. Bristol & Exeter Railway 1851.		1876
114		Exeter & Exmouth. 1846. Part built later 1857. To the South Western 1861.		
115	66	Exeter, Tiegn Valley & Chagford Railway. 1883. Revived 1897 as Exeter Railway Co. 1898. 8 miles. Worked by GWR. Opened 1905.		1923
116	30	Exe Valley Railway. 1874. Absorbed by Bristol & Exeter 1875. Built by GWR.		1876
117		Exeter, Yeovil & Dorchester. Part built later 1856 as London South Western Branch.		
118		Falmouth & Redruth Railway. 1864. Not built.		Not built
119	16	Faringdon Railway Co. Converted 1878 (3½ miles). Last BG east of Bristol.		1886
120		Ferndale & Maerdy Railway. Privately owned. Purchased by Taff Vale. 1886.		1922
121	111	Festiniog & Blaenau Railway Co. Still open as a tourist attraction (1-ft 11½-in gauge).	76	1883
122	247	Fishguard & Rosslare Railway & Harbours Co. Joint GWR & GNW Railway (Ireland).		1898
123	176	Forest of Dean Railway. 1809. Originally a tramway (Bullo Railway Act).		
	178	Forest Of Dean Central Railway Co. 1856. Opened 1868 (5 miles long) included the dissolved Bullo Tramway Co. from 1847.	39	1863
124A		Gloucester & Cheltenham Railway.	35	1836
124		Glamorgan Central Mineral Railway Co. Company defunct, not completed.		
125	181	Gloucester & Berkeley New Docks Branch Railway. 1872. Joint GWR & Midland Railways.		1894

126	144	Gloucester & Dean Forest Railway Co. 1846. Leased in perpetuity to GWR 1851.		1875
127	152	Golden Valley Railway Co. Purchased from Liquidator (18¾ miles).		1901
128		Great Western & Great Central Joint Railway.		1899
129		Great Western Union Railway.	35	1836
130	13	Great Marlow Railway Co. 1868. Worked by GWR from 1872.		1897
131	7	Great Western & Brentford Railway Co. 1855. Leased to GWR 1859.		1871
132	1	Great Western Railway Co. London to Bristol 1835.		1836
133	201	Great Western & Taff Vale Joint Railway. 1867. Opened 1877.		1923
134	8	Great Western & Uxbridge Railway Co. 2½ miles long. Built as GWR Branch.		1858
135	12	Great Western & Wycombe. 1846. Replaced by Wycombe Railway 1852. Partly GWR.		1867
136	240	Gwendraeth Valley Railway Co. Incorporated 1866. Opened 1871. Carmarthen & Cardigan Kidwelly Branch. 3 miles and two locomotives!		1923
137		Halesowen & Bromsgrove Branch Railway Co. 1865. Became...		Joint 1906
138	132	Halesowen Railway Co. 1876. Worked with Midland from 1872. Opened 1883.		
139	2	Hammersmith & City Railway Co. 1861. Joint with Metropolitan from 1867. Electrically worked from 1906.		1864–69
140	84	Hayle Railway. 1834. Bought by West Cornwall Railway. 1846. Extended c. 1835 to Carne Brea Mines.		1876
141	187	Halls Tramroad, Abercarn Railway or Llanover Tramroad. Originally a horse tramroad. Leased to GWR for 1,000 yrs. 1877.		1877
142	85	Helston Railway Co. 1880. 8¾ miles long. Opened 1887. Worked by GWR from 1885.		1898
143		Helston & Penrhyn Railway. Not built.		Not built
144		Hereford, Hay & Brecon. 1859. Absorbed by the Midland 1886.	78	
145	147	Hereford, Ross & Gloucester Railway Co. 1851. Leased to GWR from its opening.	45	1863
146	239	Kidwelly & Burry Port Railway Co. Converted in 1865 from a canal system and amalgamating in 1866 with the Burry Port & Gwendraeth Valley Railway Co. Originally Kidwelly & Llanelly Canal & Tramroad Co. 1813.		1922
147	156	Kington & Eardisley Railway Co. 1862. Adapted from Kington Tramway. Purchased for about one-sixth cost.	46	1898
148	69	Kingsbridge & Salcombe Railway Co. 1882. Opened 1893.		1888

149	42	Lambourne Valley Railway Co. Incorporated 1883. Opened 1898 (12¼ miles long).		1905
150	174	Lampeter, Aberayron & New Quay Light Railway Co. 1906. Worked by GWR from 1909. Opened 1911.		1922
151		Landore & Swansea Vale Railway. 1850. Formed to acquire Swansea Valley Railway.		To Midland 1876
152	54	Langport & Durston Railway. GWR, 1904. Opened 1906.		1904
153	60	Launceston & South Devon Railway Co. 1862. Amalgamated with South Devon Railway 1869.		1878
154	154	Leominster & Bromyard Railway Co. 1874. Portion worked by GWR 1883.		1888
155		Leominster & Hereford Railway.		
156	155	Leominster & Kington Railway Co. Two branch Titley to Presteign. 1854. 13 miles.		1861
157	139	Lightmoor & Coalbrook Dale Railway. GWR 1861. Opened 1864.		1861
158	74	Liskeard & Caradon Railway Co. Taken over by Liskeard & Looe Co. Opened 1844 (originally horses) in 1901. From 1862 worked by Caradon Railway with locomotives until 1909. Worked by GWR from 1909.		1923 Abandoned 1931
159	75	Liskeard & Looe Railway Co. 1825 & 1858. 7 miles long originally. 1825 a Plate Railway. Incorporated L&L Union Canal Co. 1825. Worked by GWR 1909.		1923
160	75	Liskeard & Looe Union Canal Co. Railway mostly on canal site. Act for Canal 1825. Act 1858 Authorised substitution of railway for canal.		1923
161	238	Llanelly & Mynydd Mawr Railway Co. 1875. Originally the Carmarthenshire Railway Co. 1802. Plate tramroad.		1923
162	238	Llanelly Railway. Part absorbed by LNWR as Central Wales & Carmarthen Co. in 1889. Twenty-one locos 1873. Renumbered by GWR 894–914.		1889
163	236	Llanelly Railway & Dock Co. 1828. For Railway or Tramroad. Amalgamated with GWR by Act of 1189. Part to LNWR 1891.		1889
164	107	Llangollen & Corwen Railway Co. 1860. Worked by GWR from 1865 opening.		1896
165	162	Llanidloes & Newtown Railway Co. 1862. To Cambrian Railway 1864. (12¼ miles).		1922
166	206	Llantrissant & Taff Vale Junction Railway Co. 1861. Worked and leased by the Taff Vale 1889.		1922
167	187	Llanover Tram Road. See Halls Tramroad.		
168		Llynvi & Ogmore Railway Co. 1866. Llynvi Valley Railway joined the Ogmore Valley Railway 1866. Twelve locos to GWR Nos 915–926.		1873

169	217	Llynvi Valley. 1846. Amalgamated in 1866 as Llynvi & Ogmore Railway Co.	117	(1873)
170	79	Lostwithiel & Fowey Railway. 1893. Taken over by Cornwall Mineral Railway.		1896
171		Lostwithiel & Foye Railway. 1862. Closed 1879. Originally broad gauge. Reopened by GWR 1895 as standard gauge.		1895
172	158	Ludlow & Clee Hill Railway Co. 1861. To Shrewsbury & Hereford, then jointly with L&NW Railway.		1893
173	179	Lydney & Lydbrook. 1809. Integrated with Severn & Wye Railway & Canal 1810. Joint with GWR & Midland, 1894.	39	1894
174		Lydney & Barnstaple. 1898. A narrow gauge 1 ft 11½ in. Sold to Southern Railway. A minor thorn for a very short period in the side of GWR.		
175	18	Malmesbury Railway Co. 1872. 6½ miles. Half financed by GWR.		1877
176	173	Manchester & Milford Railway Co. 1860. Pencader to Aberystwyth. Leased to GWR 1906. 41½ miles. Only small portion of original idea as Manchester & Milford are about 200 miles apart!		1911
177	47	Marlborough Railway Co. Incorporated 1861. Worked by GWR from opening 1864.		1923
178	45	Marlborough & Grafton Railway. Incorporated 1896. Worked by Midland, SW Junction Railway 1896.		1923
179	171	Mawddwy Railway Co. 1865. Taken over by Cambrian Railway 1911 after closing in 1908.		1923
180		Merthyr, Tredegar & Abergavenny Railway. 1859. To London North Western 1866.	85	
181	177	Micheldean Road & Forest Of Dean Junction Railway Co. 1871.		1880
182	43/45	Midland & South Western Junction Railway Co. Incorporated 1884. Formed by Swindon, Marlborough & Andover Railway and Swindon & Cheltenham Extension Railway.		1922
183	165	Mid Wales Railway Co. 1864. Taken over by the Cambrian Railway, 1904.		1922
184	248	Milford Railway Co. Incorporated 1856. Worked by GWR from 1863 opening.		1896
185	33	Minehead Railway Co. 1871. 8½ miles long. Bristol & Exeter, 1874.		1897
186	185	Monmouthshire Canal Co. 1972. Became the Monmouthshire Railway & Canal Co. Lines worked by GWR from 1875. Railways from Act of 1802, 1845, 1848, 1852, 1853, 1865, 1874, 1875.		1880
187	185	Monmouthshire Railway & Canal Co. 1798 & 1848. Title changed from Newport & Pontypool Railway 1845 (see also Park Mile Railway).	1	1880

188	185	Monmouthshire Railway & Canal. 1845. Purchased Llanvimangel Railway 1811.	83, 5	1880
189		Grosmont Railway 1812, & Hereford Railway Co. 1826 (all distinct tramway companies).	12, 13, 15	1880
190	151	Monmouth Railway Co. 1817. Ex-plate 3-ft 6-in gauge. Absorbed by Coleford Railway 1872.		1875
199		Monmouth & Hereford Railway Co. 1845. Later constructed in part only 1855 & 1874.		1845
200	150	Monmouth & Wye Valley Railway. 1866		1885
201	64	Moretonhampstead & South Devon Railway Co. 1862. Originally Newtown & Moretonhampstead. South Devon Railway, 1866.		1876
202	234	Morriston Railway. (GWR) 1872. Extension to Swansea District line.		1872
203	137	Much Wenlock & Severn Junction Railway Co. 1852. Leased to West Midland. Worked GWR 1875. 3½ miles long.		1873
204	117	Moss Valley Railway. (GWR) 1873. Opened 1882.		1873
		Nantlle Railway. 1825. 7 miles. To Caernarvon Railway 1867. To LNW Railway 1870.		
205	103	Nantwich & Market Drayton Railway Co. 1861. Joined by Wellington & Market Drayton 1867. Worked by GWR from 1862.		1897
206	244	Narberth Road & Maenclochog Railway. 1876. Taken over by the North Pembrokeshire & Fishguard Railway in 1895, thence to GWR.		1898
207	231	Neath & Brecon Railway Co. 1863. Ex-Dulais Valley Mineral Railway 1862.	88, 90	1922
208		Neath, Pontardawe & Brynammon Railway. 1895. Constructed by GWR.		1895
209	131	Netherton & Halesowen Railway. (GWR) 1862. Two branches. 1892 & 1898.		1892 & 1898
210	146	Newent Railway Co. 1873. Opened 1885.		1892
211	123	Newport, Abergavenny & Hereford Railway Co. 1846. Absorbed Hereford Railway (Plateway) 1846. Became part of West Midland 1860.	27	1863
212	185	Newport & Pontypool Railway. 1845. Title changed to Monmouthshire Railway & Canal Co. 1848.		1880
213		Newquay Railway. Treffry Estate Tramroad (see Illustration 59).		
214	78	Newquary & Cornwall Junction Railway. 1864. Taken over by Cornwall Minerals Railway 1874. Broad & narrow gauge. 5¼ miles long.		1896
215	163	Newtown & Machynlleth Railway. Incorporated 1854. To Cambrian Railways 1864. 23 miles.		1922
216		Newtown & Moretonhampstead. 1858. Became Monmouth Railway Co.		1876
217	245	North Pembrokeshire & Fishguard Railway Co. Associated with the Fishguard & Rosslare Railway. (See also Rosebush & Fishguard.) 1878.		1898

218	105	North Wales Mineral Railway. 1844. Amalgamated to become Shrewsbury & Chester Railway 1846. To Cambrian Railway 1863.		1846
219		North Wales Railway. Not constructed. Later part built as Bangor & Carnarvon Railway.		
220		North Devon & Cornwall Junction Railway. 1925. Replaced an 1880 tramway in past, for clay traffic.		
221	219	Ogmore Valley Railway. Incorporated 1863. Joined Llynvi Valley Railway in 1866 to form Ogmore & Llynvi Valley Railway.		1873
222		Okehampton Railway. 1862. Standard gauge. Became Devon & Cornwall Railway.		To LSW Railway 1889
223	130	Oldbury Railway Co. 1873. Worked by GWR from 1876.		1894
224	160	Oswestry, Ellesmere & Whitchurch Railway. 1864. To Cambrian Railway 1864. 18 miles long.		1922
225	161	Oswestry & Newtown Railway Co. 1863. Absorbed by Cambrian Railway 1864. 30 miles long.		1922
226	87	Oxford Railway Co. 1843. Totally financed by GWR. 9½ miles.		1844
227	89	Oxford & Rugby Railway Co. 1845. Absorbed by GWR 1846.		1860
228	121	Oxford, Worcester & Wolverhampton Railway Co. 1845. Became part of West Midland Railway 1860.	32	1863
229		Par & Fowey Railway. 16½ miles.		1877
230	186	Park Mile Railway. Ex-tramroad 1805. Newport through Tredegar Estate.		1923
231	242	Pembroke & Tenby Railway. 1859. To South Wales Railway 1863. 28 miles.		1897
232	211	Penarth Extension Railway Co. 1876. (1¼ miles) Leased to Taff Vale.		1923
233	210	Penarth Harbours, Docks & Railway Co. 1857. Worked by Taff Vale.		1922
234		Pewsey & Salisbury Railway Co. 1883. Not constructed.		1884
235	See 70	Plymouth & Datmoor Railway. Tramroad converted by GWR, Bristol & Exeter and Bristol & Gloucester (see also 237 below).	54	1886
236	60	Plymouth, Devonport & Exeter Railway. Name changed to South Devon Railway 1844.		1876
237	72	Plymouth & Great Western Dock Co. 1846. Vested in Bristol & Exeter, GWR and South Devon Railway Cos. From 1874. Opened 1857.		1874
238		Plymouth & North Devon. 1895. Abandoned 1907.		
239	114	Ponky Branch Railway. GWR 1889. Opened 1861 &1875 (legalised '1889').	71	1889
240	184	Pontypool, Caerleon & Newport Railway Co. 1865. 12 miles.		1874

245	112	Pontycysyllte Railway. 1901. Purchased from Shropshire Union Railway & Canal Co.		1901
246	190	Pontypridd, Caerphilly & Newport Railway. 1878. Acquired Alexandra Dock Railway 1896.		1891/1922
247	58	Portland Breakwater Railway. 1874. GWR and L&SW Joint.		1874
248	31	Portbury Pier Railway. 1846. Became Bristol & Portishead 1863.		1876
249	222	Port Talbot Railway & Docks Co. 1894. Worked by GWR from 1908.		1922/08
250		Powlesland & Mason Railway. Purchased by GWR.		1924
251	94	Princes Risborough & Grendon Underwood Railway. 1899. GWR & GC Joint.		1906
252	70	Princetown Railway. 1878. Worked by GWR from 1883 opening. Financed by GWR (10½ miles long) and used part of old Plymouth & Dartmoor route. Closed 1956.	54	1922
253	199	Quakers Yard & Merthyr Joint Line. GWR & Rhymney Railway 1882. No locos or stock. Convenience line between Quakers Yard and Merthyr GWR. Opened 1886.		1922
254	81	Retew Branch Extension Railway. 1910. Opened 1912.		1910
255		Rhonda & Ely Valleys Junction Railway. 1845. Proposed.		Not built
256	224	Rhondda & Swansea Bay Railway Co. 1882. Workshops at Danygraig.	126	1906
257	204	Rhondda Valley & Hirwain Junction Railway Co. 1867. Absorbed by Taff Vale Railway 1884.		1922
258	194	Riverside Branch Railway. Acts 1880 & 1891.		1880
259	196	Rhymney Railway Co. 1854. Various branch openings from 1858–1906.		1922
260	197	Rhymney & LNW Joint Railway. 1864. Opened 1871.		1922
261	245	Rosebush & Fishguard Railway Co. 1878 (Changed name to North Pembrokeshire & Fishguard Railway Co. 1884.		1898
262		Northberth Road & Maenclochg Railway. 1872. Extended by R&F Railway.		
263	193	Roath Dock Branch Railway. (GWR) 1896. Opened 1903.		1896
264	145	Ross & Ledbury Railway Co. 1873. 4¾ miles. Opened 1885.		1892
265	148	Ross & Monmouth Railway Co. 1865. 12½ miles. Worked from opening by GWR.		1922
266	191	Rumney Railway Co. 1825. Integrated with Brecon & Merthyr 1863.		1922
267	228	Redruth & Chacewater Railway. 1826. Mineral line tramway. Steam from 1854. 4-ft gauge. Independent of GWR. Closed 1915.	61	1865

268	134	Severn Valley Railway Co. 1853. Leased to West Midland. 40 miles.		1863
269	179	Severn & Wye Railway & Canal Co. Became Lydney & Lyndbrook Railway Co. 1809. In 1869 developed as steam power from horse tramway of 3-ft 8-in gauge. 30 miles long. Broad gauge beside tramway until 1872.		1894
270	180	Severn Bridge Railway. Incorporated 1872. Joined with S&W Railway & Canal 1879 to form...	41	1894/1950
271	179/181	Severn & Wye & Severn Bridge Railway Co. 1879. Joint with Midland 1894, then Western Region British Rail 1950.	42	
272	101	Shrewsbury & Birmingham Railway Co. 1846. Absorbed by GWR 1854. Narrow gauge.		1863
273	104/105	Shrewsbury & Chester. 1846. Amalgamation of Shrewsbury, Oswestry & Chester Junction Railway & North Wales Mineral Railway.	52	
274	153	Shrewsbury & Hereford Railway Co. 1846. Became part of West Midland 1860, jointly with L&NW Railway.		1863
275	168	Shrewsbury & North Wales Railway Co. 1862. Later Potteries. Shrewsbury & North Wales 1864. Worked by Cambrian Railway (GWR) from 1881.		1922
276	104	Shrewsbury, Oswestry & Chester. 1845. Amalgamated to become Shrewsbury & Chester in 1846.		1846
277	159	Shrewsbury & Welshpool Railway. 1856. Joint with L&NW Railway.		1865
278	168	Shropshire Railway. Worked NNE 1862. Became No. 260. Part of Cambrian Railway 1886.		1922
279	112	Shropshire Union Railway & Canal Co. See Pontycysyllte Railway.		1896
280		Somerset Central & Dorset Central Railways. 12½ miles. Combined 1852 to form Somerset & Dorset Railway (followed by a very chequered career).	47	To the LMS&S Railway. 1923
281	60	South Devon Railway Co. 1844. Absorbed the following lines: Dartmouth & Torbay (1857) in 1864, Launceston & South Devon (1862) in 1869.	52	1878
	63	South Devon & Tavistock Railway Co. 1854 to South Devon Railway in 1865. Worked the Buckfastliegh, Totnes & South Devon Railway. Total 123½ miles.		1876 1897
282		South Wales & Great Western Direct Railway. Not built – abandoned 1870.		Not built
283	223	South Wales Mineral Railway Co. 1853. Worked by GWR from 1908.		1922/08
284	175	South Wales Railway Co. 1845. Leased by GWR 1862.		1863
285	23	South Wales & Bristol Direct Railway. Authorised 1896. Running powers with Midland.		1896

286	9	Staines & West Drayton Railway Co. 1873. Worked by FWR from 1882.		1900
287	48	Stert & Westbury Railway. (GWR) 1894. Opened 1900.		1894
288		Stonehouse & Nailsworth Railway. 1863. Continued by the Wilts & Gloucestershire. 5¾ miles.		Purchased by Midland
289	129	Stourbridge Railway Co. 1860. 3½ miles. Worked by GWR from Opening.		1870 1874
290	86	St Ives Branch Railway. 1873. Last broad gauge as new.		1878
291	126	Stratford & Moreton Railway Co. 1821. Horse tramway absorbed by Oxford, Worcester & Wolverhampton 1845.		1863
292		Stourbridge Extension Canal. 1837. Purchased by Oxford, Worcester & Wolverhampton 1846.		1863
293	96	Stratford-Upon-Avon Railway Co. 1857. 9¼ miles.		1883
294		Swansea & Amman Junction. Built later as Swansea Vale (Branch) 1847.		1922
295	229	Swansea Harbour Railway. 1857. Leased to Vale of Neath Railway 1862.		1923
	233	Swansea Harbour Trust (Docks) 1854. Leased to Vale of Neath Railway 1862.		
296	228	Swansea & Neath Railway Co. 1861. Mixed gauge. 7¾ miles. Amalgamated with Vale of Neath Railway 1863.		1865
297	230	Swansea Vale, Neath & Brecon Railway. 1864. To Neath and Brecon. Line operated by Midland Railway.		LMS/GWR
298	43	Swindon & Cheltenham Extension Railway. 1881. Amalgamated with Swindon, Marlborough & Andover as Midland & SW Junction Railway 1884.		
299	17	Swindon & Highworth Light Railway Co. 1875.		1882
300	44	Swindon, Marlborough & Andover. 1873, Became Midland & SW Junction Railway.		1923
301	167	Tanat Valley Light Railway Co. 1904. Taken over by Taff Vale Railway.		1922
302	198	Taff Bargoed Joint Railway. 1867. Opened 1875/76. GWR & Rhymney Railway.		1922
303	200	Taff Vale Railway Co. 1836. Augmented overloaded canal system. A combination of eleven companies absorbed. Total 412 miles. 1889. There were also twenty-three major branches to collieries included in the total.		1922
304	27	Taw Vale Railway. Became North Devon Railway 1851. Leased to B&E Railway.		1876
305	67	Teign Valley Railway Co. 1863. Worked by GWR and existed as a company until 1923.		1882
306	135	Tenbury & Bewdley Railway Co. 1859. To West Midlands. Joined the Severn Valley Railway Bewdley to Tenbury. 15 miles.		1869

307	157	Tenbury Railway Co. 1859. Worked by GWR.		1863
308	46	Tidworth Camp Railway. 1900. Worked by Midland & SW Junction Railway.		1923
309	37	Tiverton & North Devon Railway Co. 1875. Opened 1884.		1894
310	68	Torbay & Brixham Railway Co. 1864. 2 miles. Broad gauge. One engine (The 0-4-0 Queen).		1883
311		Torrington & Okehampton Railway. 1895. Abandoned 1907.		
312	205	Treferig Valley Railway. 1879. 3 miles. To Taff Vale 1889.		1922
313	80	Trenance Valley Railway. (GWR) 1910.		1910
314	226	Trustees of Swansea Harbour. Vale of Neath Railway.		1865
315	82	Truro & Newquay Railway. (GWR) 1897.		1897
316	11	Uxbridge & Denham Railway (GWR) 1899. Opened 1907.		1899
317	213	Vale Of Glamorgan Railway. 1889. 20 miles. Worked by Barry Railway.		1922
318	106	Vale of Llangollen Railway Co. 1859. Worked by GWR from 1860.		1896
319	226	Vale of Neath Railway Co. 1846. Eventually mixed gauge. Worked by GWR from 1865. First eight coupled locos in country. Lateral play L&T axles (invention of French man – Mons Callait) Absorbed Aberdare Valley Railway, Swansea & Neath Railway, Swansea Harbour Railway.		1865
320	172	Vale of Rheidol Light Railway Co. 1897. 1-ft 11½-in gauge. Amalgamated with Cambrian Railway 1913.		1922
321	160/165	Van Railway. 1873. Maintained and worked by the Cambrian Railway from 1896.		
322	237	Vale of Towy Railway. Incorporated 1854. Joint with LMS & LN Western Railways. 11½ miles.		1868
323	249	Victoria Station & Pimlico Railway. 1858. Victoria Station Co. was given power by this Act to provide broad gauge rails and station accommodation for GWR. Also included for any traffic was the London Chatham & Dover Railway. GWR service to Victoria Station was discontinued in 1915.		
324	15	Wallingford & Watlington Railway Co. 1864. 9 miles. Worked by GWR from 1866.		1872
325	14	Watlington & Princes Risborough Railway Co. 1869. Opened 1872.		1883
326	102	Wellington & Market Drayton Railway Co. 1862. Joined by Nantwich & Market Drayton 1867.		1877
327	140	Wellington & Severn Junction Railway Co. 1853. Opened 1857. Leased to GWR and West Midland from 1861.		1892

328	169	Welshpool & Llanfair Railway Co. 1899. Narrow 2-ft 6-in gauge. Constructed and worked by Cambrian Railway. Opened 1903.	77	1922
329	138	Wenlock Railway Co. 1861. Worked by GWR from 1864.		1896
330	83	West Cornwall Railway Co. 1846. Leased by GWR, Bristol & Exeter, & South Devon 1865. Absorbed Hayle Railway 1846. 36¼ miles.		1878
331	4	West London Estension Railway. 1859. Incorporated by GWR, LNW Railway, South Western, LB&SC Railway.		1859
332	3	West London Railway. 1836. Original name Bristol, Birmingham & Thames Junction Railway. Vested in GWR and LNW Railway 1854.		1854
333	121 122 123	West Midland Railway Co. 1860. Incorporated the Worcester & Hereford Railway, the Abergavenny & Hereford Railway and Oxford, Worcester & Wolverhampton Railway.		1863
334	168	West Shropshire Mineral Railway. 1862. Became Shrewsbury & North Water Railway 1864. Part operated by Cambrian Railway after being derelict for some years (see also 260 and 263).		1922
335	57	Weymouth & Portland Railway. 1862. Joint GWR and Southern Railway. Also the associated Breakwater Line 1875 built and worked by GWR & LSW Railway.		1862 1874
336	34	West Somerset Railway Co. 1857. Company existed to 1922. Worked and leased to Bristol & Exeter Railway 1862 on perpetual lease.		1922
337	243	Whitland & Cardigan Railway Co. 1869. Ex-Whitland & Taff Vale Railway 1869. Worked by GWR from 1883.		1890
338		Whitland, Cronware & Pendine Railway. 1877. Not built – abandoned 1892		Not built
339		Wilts & Gloucestershire Railway Co. 1869. A continuation of the Stonehouse & Nailsworth Railway.		Not built
340	49	Wilts, Somerset & Weymouth Railway Co. 1845. Absorbed by GWR 1851. Proposed as Wilts & Somerset Railway.		1851
341	90	Witney Railway Co. 1859. Yarnton to Witney. 8 miles. Leased to West Midland 1860, then GWR from 1873. Opened 1861.		1890
342		Windsor & Ascot Railway. 1898. Dissolved 1901. Abandoned 1904.		1898
343	92	Woodstock Railway Co. 1886. Purchased for £15,000. Worked by GWR from 1889.		1897
344	127	Worcester, Bromyard & Leominster Railway Co. 1861. Half abandoned, became Leominster & Bromyard. Line worked and maintained by GWR. Opened 1874.		1888

345		Worcester, Dean Forest & Monmouth Railway. 1863. Not built.		Not built
346	122	Worcester & Hereford Railway Co. 1853. Became part of West Midland 1860. Opened 1859.		1863
347	115	Wrexham & Mineral Railway. 1861		1871
348	166	Wrexham & Ellsmere Railway Co. 1885. Line worked by Cambrian Railway 1891.		1922
349	116	Wrexham & Mineral Extension Railway. 1865. Joint GWR & LRW Railway. Opened 1872.		1866
350	35	Wrington Vale Light Railway. (GWR) 1898. Opened 1901. 6½ miles.		1898
351	12	Wycombe Railway Co. 1846. Broad gauge altered to narrow (Act 1846) in 1870. Opened 1854. Closed for goods traffic 1967, passengers 1970.		1867
352	150	Wye Valley Railway Co. 1866. Worked by GWR from opening 1876.		1905
353	71	Yealmpton Railway. 1888. Authority to make line, which had no direct connection with the GWR, transferred from Plymouth & Dartmoor Railway by Act of 1892. Access by running powers over Southern Railway (original Act Plymouth & Dartmoor Railway 1888).		1892

Who Had A Red Face!?

Having looked through the foregoing list of railway companies which came into being throughout the growth years of the Great Western Railway alone, a critic, writing in the *Quarterly Review* of c. 1829 proclaimed:

> As to those persons who speculate on making railways generally throughout the Kingdom, and superseding all the canals, all the wagons, mail and stage coaches, post chaises, and in short every other mode of conveyance by land and by water, we deem them and their visionary schemes unworthy of notice. The gross exaggerations of the powers of the locomotive steam engine (or to speak in plain English, the 'Steam Carriage',) may delude for a time, but must end in the mortification of those concerned. We should as soon expect people to suffer themselves to be fired off upon one of Congreve's rockets*, as trust themselves to the mercy of such a machine, going at such a rate! Engines travelling at rates up to 20 miles per hour? Nothing can do more harm towards their general adoption and improvement than the promulgation of such nonsense!

---

* Military explosive projectile

The 1922 Amalgamation

The last attempt, short of 'Nationalisation', to affect some form of 'standardisation'. Whilst the requirements of amalgamation must have caused considerable administration difficulties for all involved, not only the Great Western but in all of the other constituent companies throughout the country, it must have been a fascinating period on the works side.

In the case of the Great Western Railway (GWR), to suddenly receive the responsibility for upward of a thousand locomotives for maintenance, on top of existing stock requirements, opened a new field of work. The inherited engines were, in most cases, not of GWR design or original build, coming from a number of contractors. Standards of maintenance varied from almost none to excellent depending on the facilities of the absorbed companies, and the position of the loco on the maintenance schedule when it was taken over. With limited funds and facilities, the maintenance, particularly if by contract because of limited facilities at the home base, had to be carefully arranged on the financial side by the company concerned, and was conditioned also by the resentment to take over by the GWR.

From the GWR point of view, it now had to examine all of the stock absorbed, and sort the wheat from the chaff with regard to those locomotives which would be retained, those which required work to be done (which was the majority), and those which, because of design or condition, would not fit the required standards or application, and were to be scrapped or sold as soon as possible.

To assist with a measure of standardisation, those locomotives which were considered acceptable would be 'Westernised' – or more correctly 'Swindonised' – usually with the fitting of as many Great Western components as possible. The earlier introduction of the range of Churchward standard boilers and fittings formed the greatest pool of replacement, and a large number of absorbed locomotives when shopped for overhaul over the following years were fitted with one of the series of boilers and fittings, giving them a hybrid Great Western look.

All of this work was required on top of the routine continuing output, of the programme of new and repaired GWR engines from the main works at Swindon. The absorbed stock was mostly small-type tank locomotives, even the limited number of tender 'passenger' types taken over were generally of 0-6-0 or similar small wheel base format, and most of these only lasted a few more years.

An exclusion to this is of course the locomotives from another source, but absorbed at the same period. These were the Railway Operating Division (or ROD) locomotives, purchased or hired around the same period from the Government. These locomotives had either been destined for 'the Western Front' and its environs in the late First World War, or had actually been returned from such service and offered for sale.

These large 2-8-0 tender engines varied from literally new to well used, and added to the workflow through the shops. Those that survived scrutiny were repaired and maintained to Swindon standards, but were among those which were not 'Swindonised', retaining their original appearance to the end. They lasted well, and it was considerably after the Second World War and into the 'Nationalisation' period of the '40s and '50s when the last went to the scrap yard. I remember, as an apprentice (1946–51) working with a fitter on repair of one of these locomotives, some of the difficulties of removing items. The fitter insisted that 'even the b— bolts and nuts were case hardened!'

All 'accepted' locomotives had a general arrangement drawing of their type prepared at the Swindon Drawing Office, the three-view drawing known as a 'diagram' and identified by a letter.

A short note on each of the absorbed companies and its stock follows, listed in descending order of total locomotive stock involved.

The Companies Absorbed 1921–24
Constituent and Subsidiary (Total 18 Companies)

No.	NAME	ABSORBED	No. OF LOCOS
1	Taff Vale Railway	1 Jan 1922	275
2	Barry Railway	1 Jan 1922	148
2	Rhymney Railway	1 Jan 1922	123
4	Cambrian Railways including:	1 Jan 1922	99
	Vale of Rheidol (1-ft 11-in gauge)		3
	Welshpool & Llanfair (2-ft 6-in gauge)		2
5	Brecon & Merthyr Railway	1 July 1922	47
6	Alexandra Docks Railway	1 Jan 1922	39
7	Rhondda & Swansea Bay Railway	1 Jan 1922	37
8	Cardiff Railway	1 Jan 1922	36
9	Midland & South Western Junction Railway	1 July 1923	29
10	Port Talbot Railway	1 Jan 1922	22
11	Burry Port & Gwendraeth Railway	1 July 1922	15
12	Neath & Brecon Railway	1 July 1922	15
13	Swansea Harbour Trust	1 July 1923	14
14	Powlesland & Mason Railway	1 Jan 1924	9
15	Llanelly & Mynydd Mawr Railway	1 Jan 1923	8
16	South Wales Mineral Railway	1 Jan 1923	5
17	Cleobury Mortimer & Ditton Priors Light Railway	1 Jan 1922	2
18	Gwendraeth Valleys Railway (included in 11 above)	1 Jan 1923	2

Several of the larger companies absorbed were, like the Great Western Railway itself, hybrids, having absorbed or been involved with other companies in the span of their histories, often as long as the Great Western's.

1 – Taff Vale Railway

This formed certainly the largest of the railways absorbed by the GWR at this time, bringing 275 locomotives under the Great Western control.

The Taff Vale was almost as old as the Great Western itself, being in its own right a successful undertaking, and following closely, by only a few months, after the GWR had obtained its Act of Incorporation in 1836. Its first line opened in 1840 from Cardiff to Merthyr, and within twenty years its branches had spread from the main lines to total about 90 miles of track. Indeed, initially, it had the same engineer (IKB) as the Great Western.

Associated also with dock working at Penarth Dock, with an additional rail link, it had earlier, in 1889, taken over and absorbed the Llantrisant and Taff Vale Junction Railway. Its success continued right up to takeover by the GWR when almost 120 miles of track including over 20 miles of four-track route were included, with the extensive and varied stock.

Mostly tank engines were involved, both pannier and saddle types, with wheel arrangements including 0-4-0, 0-6-2, 4-4-0, 4-4-2 and 0-6-0. The latter arrangement also applied to eighty-five tender engines of 'L' class, forty-three of which survived the grouping, changed to 'K' class as a selected number were progressively rebuilt with a more powerful boiler, in the 'Swindonisation' programme, applied to many absorbed engines from many sources. Like the majority of absorbed engines, however, they had all gone to the scrap yard within fifteen years.

The remaining locomotives were mostly 0-6-2 tanks from various makers. Kitsons, Neilson Reids, Hudswell Clarke, Manning Wardle, Hawthorn Leslie, North British Loco and Vulcan Foundry, in fact from such a large stud of locomotives, most of the well-known manufacturers are represented. A rather rare event for the 'grouping', was the very long rebuild programme of the batch of '04' series 0-6-2s, lasting until 1946 when the last was reboiled (to Swindon practice), with No. 3 boilers!

There were many problems in absorbing the small railways of the 'grouping', a grouping not really wanted by the GWR in the first place. The railways had their own local problems, and among those on the Taff Vale was the 'Pwllryhebog Incline', the track length which served the Clydach Vale Colliery. Not least of the difficulties was the pronunciation of Welsh place names!

Ordered from Kitsons in 1884 were the three special engines to work the colliery coal traffic up and down the incline, 1:13 to start with then easing to 1:30. These locomotives were certainly internally different as regards the boiler, although externally appearing as ordinary 0-6-0 side tanks with possibly larger wheels than would be expected for the nature of their work.

The boilers had very noticeable taper on the middle ring and sloping crowns to the fireboxes to ensure adequate water cover when on the incline, with very high domes mounted above the firebox for the collection of steam that was as dry as possible as there were no superheater arrangements. The safety valves were positioned on top of the dome. In use, the locos worked attached to a steel cable which passed over a wheel at the top of the incline and was attached to a descending train of trucks, thus the weight of the train ascending with the empties, acted as a brake for the full trucks descending, and was also assisted in its own ascent by the weight of the descending full trucks.

Joining the 0-6-0s at the top of the incline were a couple of Hudswell Clarke 0-4-0 shunters, very minute engines weighing only just of 11 tonnes and built in 1876. Both had been scrapped before 1930.

Passenger traffic was handled by half a dozen 4-4-2s built around 1890 by the Vulcan Foundry, assisting the three 4-4-0s, built in 1884 to handle branch line traffic. The latter were used very effectively (and were re-boilered to increase power), for auto-engine traffic, where trailer coaches could be controlled either from the locomotive or from the coach at the opposite end of the train. The 4-4-2s and 4-4-0s lasted only until the late 1920s after being taken over on grouping.

2 – The Barry Railway Company

Following development of the Penarth and Cardiff Docks for export of coal, the existing rail facilities were quickly found to be inadequate to handle the huge quantities involved. The Taff Vale and the Cardiff rail systems struggled manfully but could not cope, so, following the Act of 1884, the Barry Dock and Railway Company started operating in 1888, eventually using 148 steam locomotives, coming second in total locomotives to the Taff Vale itself.

Connecting with the Taff Vale, a mineral line from Tanteg Junction to Treforest Junction carried mineral traffic, and the main line from Cadoxton also connected with the Taff Vale at Trhafod Junction, the latter adding about 19 miles to the system.

Passenger traffic from and to Barry Island for the steamer service was also included, and in total, with special running agreements over the Brecon and Merthyr metals, about 65 miles of track were involved in the system.

At the peak of coal traffic, around the beginning of the First World War, the tonnage of coal moved from mines to docks per year was about 10–11 million tonnes.

3 – The Rhymney Railway Company

Joined to the Taff Vale lines at the delightfully named Walnut Tree Junction, the Rhymney Railway was first tracked from Rhymney to Mengoed, always with the intention of running through Cardiff. Difficulties with the TVR held up the latter until 1858, and although running powers were reluctantly granted, a new direct line from Rhymney via Caerphilly and Llanishen was sanctioned in 1864, opening in 1871 to Cardiff.

The Rhymney was certainly a 'running powers' advocate, having such leads into many of the industries and collieries in its area, covered by branches from its 51 track miles. The Caerphilly association developed into that of a major repair works in 1925, taking stock for area repair without the 'Swindon' involvement for its 123 locomotives passed over at the time of the grouping.

Most of the stock of 0-6-2T configuration with about fifteen 0-6-0 and five 2-4-2 types. The most conspicuous change was to that of the GWR taper boiler applied in a number of cases. The 2-4-2s, incidentally, built by the Vulcan Foundry, did not last long in GWR ownership, being scrapped in 1928.

Two odd-looking locomotives which only just survived to receive their GWR numbers were the tractor units built by Hudswell Clarke in 1907 for the 'rail motors', a sort of self-propelled carriage-cum-steam-loco. Originally 0-4-0 with outside cylinders, they were made into 0-4-2 tanks because of rough riding difficulties. Separated from the carriage, with a bunker extension and another pair of coupled wheels they were changed yet again into 0-6-0 locos in their own right. They had a shorter 'grouped' life than even the Vulcan 2-4-2s, being cut up in 1925.

4 – The Cambrian Railway

Passing through very scenic countryside, the 300 miles of Cambrian track and 107 locomotives taken over by GWR at the 'Amalgamation' in 1922 was itself the result of earlier amalgamations.

In 1865, a combining of four small railway companies, Oswestry & Newton Railway, Llanidloes & Newtown Railway, Newtown & Machynlleth and the Aberystwyth & Welsh Coast Railway, all only a few years old, formed the nucleus of the system. This association was followed by inclusion of the Mid Wales Railway in 1904, and the narrow gauge metals of the Welshpool and Llanfair at 2-ft 6-in gauge and the Vale of Rheidol tracks, the latter to 1-ft 11½-in gauge.

The main Cambrian Workshops were at Oswestry, retained in the scheme of things as a major workshop, and superceding Shrewsbury when the amalgamation took place. 'Oswestry' became the name of the division when the nine 'divisions' of the GWR were formed to handle running and maintenance of the system.

A very varied locomotive stock consisted mainly of 0-6-0 and 4-4-0 tender types with a sprinkling of 2-4-0 and six Beyer-Peacock 4-4-0 outside cylinder tank engines with a distinctly 'Continental' look, the latter scrapped almost immediately on takeover as not effective and not worth rebuilding. The 107 locomotives taken over were quickly examined and the total stock reduced within a year to eight-four, by condemning a varied twenty-three to start with.

Included with the Cambrian stock were the locomotives of the 1-ft 11½-in gauge Vale of Rheidol Railway, a small line of almost 12 miles from Aberystwyth to Devils Bridge. Originally three locos were running; the smallest of the three, a 2-4-0 by Bagnalls was withdrawn in 1924. The other two larger engines by Davies and Metcalfe (shades of injector manufacture) were augmented by two more built to almost identical designs at Swindon and running right into British Rail days, being among the last steam engines to be so maintained.

Another small associated railway run by the Cambrian was that of the Welshpool and Llanfair which had about 9 miles of 2-ft 6-in gauge track. The only stock was Beyer-Peacock, two locomotives built in 1902 and rebuilt at Swindon in 1930 with the usual new boilers. In 1956 both engines were 'mothballed' in store at Oswestry, but 'Preservation Societies' have now sprung up like flowers in a steam wilderness, and the Welshpool and Llanfair has blossomed again under the auspices of a preservation society, both engines being alive again.

5 – The Brecon & Merthyr Railway

Opened a little later than the original 'Railway Boom' lines, the Brecon and Merthyr was also an 'amalgamator' in its early years. Opening its first single line track in 1863 from Merthyr to Pant, it absorbed, later the same year, the Rumney Railway tracks from Bassaleg to Rhymney. The Brecon and Merthyr also had running powers over the lines of the Monmouthshire Railway & Canal Company to Newport. Branches were opened to Merthyr, again in 1863, and a line to Dowlais from Pant was opened in the following year.

A long loop to Machen, built in 1891, extended an 1864 line and immeasurably improved connections to Caerphilly, and it was at Machen that the workshop facilities were developed. The lines had a mileage of 47 and handed over a locomotive for each mile on amalgamation in 1922.

The stock was an extremely mixed bag of tank engines by a number of makers. The usual wheel arrangements included 0-6-0s by Fowler, Stephenson, Sharp Stewart, Kitson, Nasmyth Wilson, Kerr Stewart, and even the GWR. A few – three 0-6-2 tanks by Vulcan and fourteen by Stephenson – were stabled along with five 2-4-0s by Stephenson and a solitary 4-4-2 with outside cylinders by Beyer-Peacock. The latter was built in 1879 as a 4-4-0, then altered to 4-4-2 arriving on the Brecon and Merthyr after changing hands several times. She did not survive the amalgamation and a journey to Swindon Works in 1922 was her last.

The two Sharp Stewart 0-6-0s were originally saddle tanks, but were converted to pannier tank with GWR fittings in the 'Great Westernising' process which followed amalgamation. This process, which included re-boiling some of the larger 0-6-0s and 0-6-2s with standard tapered boilers, went some way toward easing maintenance and spares problems inherent in mixed loco groups.

6 – Alexandra (Newport & South Wales) Docks & Railway

This company was already a hybrid when taken over at the Grouping by the GWR. Originally, the Alexandra (Newport) Dock Company was the initiator of the Docks at Newport, that being its, at that time, sole purpose, with a link line possibly to the Great Western system.

The docks took a long time to materialise; ten years was to elapse before the first was ready. The problem of coal transport from the Rhondda and Aberdare mines to the dock was solved three years later in 1878, by the little Pontypridd, Caerphilly & Newport Railway, which itself had some difficulties. To get to Newport, the metals of the Rhymney Railway and of the Brecon & Merthyr Railway had to be used.

By 1897, there were a hundred miles of lines around the docks and sidings, and the Docks Company had absorbed the Pontypridd, Caerphilly and Newport, with almost 10 miles of running road from the Pontypridd Tramroad to join up with the Rhymney Railway at Penrhos.

Quite an array of locomotives came and went over the years before grouping, as many as fifty-six held at one time, including two special rail motors. However, by the time of the grouping, the total had reduced to thirty-nine, but what a varied lot they were! From two very model-worthy and photogenic 0-4-0s named *Trojan* and *Alexandra* from the firm of Dunn & Shute purchased in 1903, they ranged up to three odd-looking outside framed 0-6-4 side tanks built by Beyer-Peacock in 1885.

In between, the range included six Beyer-Peacock 2-6-2 side tanks, which came almost gift wrapped when in 1903 the Mersey Railway electrified and so sold off its steam stock. One of these was eventually 'Swindonised' by replacement of the boiler, appearing, apart from the retained cylindrical outside cylinders and very curved down swept steam pipes very like an ordinary GWR 2-6-2. Another 2-6-2 from the Mersey sale was a Kitson, looking very like the Beyer-Peacocks.

There was the usual sprinkling of o-6-o tanks by Stephenson, Hawthorne Leslie, R. W. Hawthorn, Peckett – very small, neat and efficient – and a couple from GWR itself. All of these were from various dates, the very rare purchase from new by the ADR being a pair of 1884 Hawthorns, and one from Stephenson's a year later and built with double frames.

The o-6-2 locos of the Alexandra Docks & Railway were comparatively heavy, long, saddle tanks with outside cylinders, those from Andrew Barclay being about 53 tonnes, purchased when coal traffic had increased at the docks, around 1908. One o-6-2 side tank dated from 1868 and began life as a o-6-o with double frames, built by the Worcester Engine Company for the Metropolitan Railway. Sold to the Sirhowy Railway in 1873, it was again put on the market and was purchased by Alexandra Docks & Railway in 1879. Rebuilt and re-boilered several times afterwards, she was finally rebuilt by Hawthorn Leslie in 1921 as a o-6-2. She lasted only six years in GWR ownership after grouping, being cut up in 1928. A number of 'grouping locos' suffered this fate. At this rather depressed time, unwanted engines were put on the 'for sale' list, and those unsold were scrapped.

Most locomotives received some attention at Swindon, and modifications of some sort, usually in the standardisation of fittings. The Kerr Stuart o-6-os were the longest survivors of the Alexandra Docks & Railway. Purchased in 1920 from the builders, they were part of a Railway Operating Division order for the Army in the late war, for which they were too late. Both lasted well into 'Nationalisation', being withdrawn in the mid-1950s.

7 – Rhondda and Swansea Bay Railway

The 29 miles of track of the Rhondda and Swansea Bay Railway were the result, with the progressive additions, of an Act initiated in 1882, long after the first rosy flush of the railway 'boom' years.

Associated inevitably with the famous 'Rhondda' coalfields, this mineral railway was first and foremost to move the black output from the mines to the docks at Port Talbot, with a later connection to the Swansea Docks. Around 1890 a connection to the metals of the Taff Vale Railway increased the contact into the coalfields when running powers were granted over the Taff Vale tracks. A short branch to Neath was the last addition, and thirty-seven locomotives covered the 29 miles of dock and running track.

The engine stock was on a par to others of the amalgamation period. The usual o-6-2 side tanks by various makers, Beyer-Peacock, Kitson and the GWR itself. The latter had already had a hand in rebuilding some of the stock a number of years before amalgamation, the main replacement being that of the boilers and boiler fittings to Great Western standard items.

Of the three 2-4-2s by Kitson used for passenger hauling, one was rebuilt with a Swindon No. 5 boiler, looking a little overbalanced on its rather strangely arranged wheelbase. Alterations to o-6-2s by Kitson were also proposed with standard boilers, No. 5s again, but this was not carried to a conclusion, so the locos ran their course with only minor alterations.

Only a couple of GWR-built Deans survived the Second World War period, being scrapped in the 1940s, all of the others of the Rhondda & Swansea Bay Railway had taken the last journey to the scrap yard by 1939.

8 – The Cardiff Railway Company

This was really a railway which wasn't a railway, in that its mileage in terms of an actual 'route' was less than 9 miles, but its associated sidings added up eventually to approximately 120 miles.

Originally controlled by the Bute family, and opened by the Marquess in 1839, it transported coal from the Bute Collieries to Bute West Dock. Until about 1860 the Taff Vale Railway supplied the motive power, when the Marquess decided to use his own engines for shunting purposes. Over the next twenty years or so, the development first of Penarth Dock and later the much larger Barry Dock took an ever increasing amount of the coal traffic away from the Bute Dock system.

Just before the turn of the century, in 1897, a new name, 'The Cardiff Railway Company' was adopted and, with the spread of sidings and loops and linking lines improved transporting and handling of coal was achieved.

On amalgamation, the locomotives involved included 0-4-0, 0-6-0, 0-6-2 and 2-4-2 types; all tank engines, several built by Kitson and Co., including the 0-4-0 saddle tanks which had a Walschaert gear variation in the form of the Hawthorn-Kitson gear, distinctive by its vertical links above the running board. Another feature of this loco was that although it carried saddle type water tanks, it had no coal bunker provision, replenishment being from a dockside stockpile when required, a little inconvenient for the fireman!

Another Kitson was an 0-6-2 with full-length side tanks, and a 'Duke' style type of boiler, with chimney, centre dome, and safety valve cover. One of these was given a GWR taper boiler which certainly in this case improved appearance.

Just two years before amalgamation, Hudswell Clarke & Co. supplied four 0-6-0 type saddle tanks which eventually were 'Swindonised' by being given a No. 11 boiler, new bunker and pannier tanks.

Engines were often altered beyond all original recognition. An example of this is with 0-6-0 GWR No. 695. Records are a little vague, but she may have been built by Beyer-Peacock about 1878 as a 0-4-2 tank, then rebuilt in 1883 to a 2-4-2 ST, and rebuilt again in 1885 as 0-6-0 T. By the early 1890s she contained a number of components from other engines in an almost complete rebuild once again.

Most locomotives were re-boiled during their careers, with standard tube renewals when required. New cylinders were often a requirement during heavy overhaul and wheel tyres received regular routine attention including re-profiling and re-tyreing.

9 – The Midland & South Western Junction Railway

As mentioned earlier in this book, 'Amalgamations' were not confined to 1922, but had always existed in the railway world. To get to Southampton from the Cheltenham–Gloucester area entailed a rather round about sort of journey, a journey eased by the linking of two railways and the acquisition of running power over the metals of the GWR.

In 1884, the Swindon, Marlborough & Andover Railway combined with the equally small Swindon & Cheltenham Extension Railway, and the merged lines, which now formed the Midland & South Western Junction Railway later opened through to Andoversford.

With the running powers over the GWR to Cheltenham, this greatly increased the Cheltenham/Southampton routing facility, linking the GWR, Midland and London & South Western Railway companies in a connecting network.

Although the usual mixed batch of twenty-nine locomotives were handed over in 1922, there were some quite distinctive locos present in the batch. A pair of o-6-o side tanks by Dubs were included, the rest were 4-4-o North British, 2-4-o Dubs, and o-6-o and 2-6-o Beyer-Peacock tender engines, and finally a couple of 4-4-4 tanks by Sharp Stewart, and an o-4-4 by Beyer-Peacock.

An 1895 pair of 2-6-o outside cylindered Beyer-Peacocks, destined originally for South America, added a Latin flavour to the loco stock, but only one, No. 16, survived to the amalgamation, the other, No. 14, being sold out of service for colliery use. The survivor was considerably altered when taken over, being given the usual treatment of a Swindon boiler, (No. 9 in this case) complete with GWR fittings, a GWR style cab, and a standard 2,500-gallon tender. Thus with a lost Latin look she ran for only about five more years before being scrapped in 1930.

The Sharp Stewart 4-4-4 tanks had similar treatment, and were fitted with No. 10 boilers, making quite handsome if unusual 'Great Western' engines. The Great Westernising process was indeed applied to the Beyer-Peacock o-6-os, (which with new boilers looked like the 22XX class), and also the 4-4-os which, after treatment and losing their twin domed parallel boilers, had somewhat of the ghost of the 'bulldogs' in their appearance, with a 'City of Truro' touch. The 4-4-os were unnamed of course, but had now 'right-hand drive' in GWR style, the controls moving over at the time of installation of the No. 2 boiler.

There is now a thriving preservation group busily re-establishing a section of the Midland & South Western Junction Railway under the name of the Swindon/Cricklade Railway, and open to the public. All volunteers, they maintain and operate steam and diesel locomotives on a track slowly approaching Swindon in one direction and Cricklade in the other.

There is currently a project just started, to build a replica of 2-6-o No. 16 which, when used on the GWR obtained the nickname of 'Galloping Gertie' due to the small driving wheels, and was originally supplied by Beyer-Peacock Loco Engineers.

10 – The Port Talbot Railway & Docks Company

Differing from the Swansea Dock Railway, whose lines did not really go anywhere except around the Docks complex, the Port Talbot Railway had tracks which snaked off from the docks into and up the valleys right to the heart of the coalfields.

The company was virtually solely concerned with the movement of the extensive coal traffic to and from the docks. The lines were slowly extended to cover a considerable area, in 1898 linking with the GWR at Pontyrhyll Junction and later also with the GWR at Pyle and Cefn Junction. The South Wales Mineral Railways and the Rhondda & Swansea Bay line were also linked in by braches connecting to Whitworth and Blaenavon.

The typical mixed batch of locomotives came over in 1922 to the GWR. The Usual 0-6-0 and 0-6-2 tanks by Stephenson and Hudswell Clarke, a 2-4-2 and 2-4-0 tanks by Sharp Stewart and five heavy 0-2-2s. These latter emerged, or at least the first two emerged, in 1899, having been purchased from the Cooke Locomotive Company of Paterson, New Jersey, being shipped as a 'kit', and put together in Barry Works. Three more were built by Sharp Stewart in 1901 to generally the same design, which at 76 tonnes were certainly the heaviest five on the Port Talbot metals.

Inevitably 'Swindonised', they were certainly different. A 'South American' looking front end with outside cylinders with box-like steam chests and valves over, surmounted by a GWR smoke box and taper boiler with copper-topped chimney, made a very distinctive diagram.

11 – The Burry Port & Gwendraeth Valley Railway Company

This long-titled railway was the most westerly of the mineral lines of South Wales, and followed the route of the old established Kymer's Canal, running through the valley bottom from Burry Port on the coast up to Cwm Mawr. The canal, one of the first canals in Wales, was constructed to take coal and limestone from the collieries and quarries of the Kymer family, 3½ miles from the coast. Established in 1769, it superseded the unreliable river transport and the time-consuming pack mule trains used to move minerals.

Missing the railway boom years, being established around 1865 the railway comprised the very much earlier components of harbour, canal, and plate tramway, a Canal Extension Act of 1812, permitting the development of either canal or plate tramway as considered appropriate.

Returning to the railway, several small branches were subsequently opened, one joining the Llanelly & Mynydd Mawr Railway in 1891, but initially for transport of minerals only. It was not until 1909 that passenger traffic was authorised, starting over part of the system from the Port to Pontyberem and later on up the valley to Cwm Mawr.

On commencing passenger traffic, more locomotives were required, and for this purpose nine side tank outside cylindered 0-6-0s were purchased from Hudswell Clarke, one of which was named 'Pioneer', its plate mounted on the side tanks.

The remaining locos, all 0-6-0s, were splendid little saddle tanks by Avonside, Chapman, and one by Hudswell Clarke. All were retained as saddle tanks, but with standard GWR fittings where appropriate, and all were originally named. Under GWR control some 'moved around' the system, from the docks at Weymouth, to Cathays, and to Taunton, where their compactness and short wheel base could be used to advantage.

Progressively withdrawn, the last to go steamed until the mid-1950s.

Two locomotives of the 'Gwendrawth Valley' portion of the company were not absorbed until six months after the Burry Port Group. Again o-6-o type saddle tank *Velindre*, a Hudswell Clarke built in 1905 was renamed *Kidwelly* before the Grouping. The second loco, *Margaret*, was an oldie by Fox-Walker, built originally for the North Pembrokeshire and Fishguard Railway and purchased from the GWR in 1911. This engine was sold, virtually on takeover, to the Kidwelly Tinplate Co. lasting into the 1950s.

12 – The Neath & Brecon Railway

The Neath & Brecon Railway at the grouping ran for about eight years under the auspices of the London Midland & Scottish Railway, having previously had association with the old Midland Railway.

Approved in 1863 and opened in 1867 the line ran from, obviously, Neath to Brecon, with a branch to Ynys-y-Geinon Junction, for the routing of through trains to Swansea, by agreement with the Swansea Vale Railway. In 1874, the Midland Railway, with an agreement to also operate over the Neath and Brecon metals, absorbed the Swansea Vale Railway, hence the Midland association, which continued for a period after the official takeover by the GWR in 1922.

Locomotives passed onto the GWR included eight o-6-o saddle tanks by Avonside Engine Co., Nasmyth Wilson, and the GWR itself, the latter responsible for four of the eight. Just after the turn of the century, Stephensons built the last three of the five o-6-2 side tank locos, all of which were withdrawn by 1931. One 2-4-o by Sharp Stewart and a 4-4-o by Yorkshire Engine Co. completed the list of Neath & Brecon Railway stock.

The latter was a neat looking side tank with outside cylinders and no cab when first constructed in 1871. After modifications around 1895 she sported a new boiler and closed cab, which made operating a more comfortable proposition for the crew. Given minor modifications, such as chimney and GWR pattern safety valves, on grouping, she lasted only about four years being withdrawn in 1926.

13 – The Swansea Harbour Trust

This was one of those railways which had no main line, and did not really go anywhere. The Swansea Harbour Trust had been running for about fifty years, having been initiated in 1854, when the Trustees decided to run things by themselves and not rely on contractors. A number of contractors had succeeded one another, with varying degrees of success, in running a system purely designed for the loading and unloading of cargoes arriving at the Swansea Docks complex.

The fourteen locomotives handed over at the amalgamation comprised 0-4-0s and 0-6-0s, the three latter quite heavy tanks by Peckett, and the small 0-4-0s by Hudswell Clarke, A. Barclay, Hawthorn Leslie, and again, Peckett.

Apart from altered lettering, through GWR to British Rail days, and the use of the GWR chimney, the little group lasted their days almost unaltered. The *King George V* locomotive, pride of the GWR, was not the only one to sport a bell! The dock engines also carried a small warning bell in front of the cab on top of the saddle tank.

The 'Small Fry' of the Amalgamation

Included in the Amalgamation were some rather miniscule railways which the Great Western would have rather done without! In fact it is quite likely the whole of the 'amalgamation' process could have been done without if the GWR had had a choice! Otherwise it would have probably 'absorbed', in one way or another, all of the Welsh companies long before the 1922 grouping! There were standard gauge companies which had less than ten locomotives, quite apart from the narrow gauges (1 ft 11½ in) of the Vale of Rheidol and the 2 ft 6 in of the Welshpool and Llanfair, both part of the Cambrian.

With a total of nine locomotives, the Powlesland & Mason Railway (14) heads the small list. If you look at a map of South Wales, you will not find the two names anywhere as they are not place names, but those of two gentlemen, the first of whom founded the company in 1865, then joined by the second in 1875.

The locomotives worked on an agency basis for the GWR on the metals of the Swansea Harbour Trust, the really tiny 0-4-0 saddle tanks only puffing around the docks area. The locos were from varied sources, four by Peckett, two from Brush Electric, one by Barclay, one from Hawthorn Leslie, and one from Avonside. The youngest dated from 1916 in the First World War years, and the eldest from 1874.

The latter had an interesting career. Starting life as one of four broad gauge engines for the South Devon Railway, being altered by the GWR two years later to narrow (4 ft 8½ in) gauge, and then being purchased by the Powlesland & Mason Railway. Rather late in the amalgamation, 1924, she came back again to the GWR, a strange-looking little engine with double coil springs over her tiny wheels, and a saddle tank that stopped short a foot or so in front of the round topped firebox and its tall safety valve cover.

One of the Brush Electric 0-4-0 saddle tanks was given the Swindon treatment and emerged in 1926 as a very much 'Swindon' looking 0-4-0 pannier tank, with a 13XX class boiler, outside cylinders and a very photogenic, model makers appearance.

Next on the list with eight locomotives is the Llanelly & Mynydd Mawr Railway (15), privately owned by a Mr Waddell, who set up the line in 1883. Based on an old plate tramway, originating from 1806, Mr Wadell agreed to rebuild his line, provide all rolling stock, and operate the complete concern for a share of the receipts.

The small mix of 0-6-0 tank engines were one each from Andrew Barclay, Manning-Wardle, Avonside, and Fox Walker, and four from Hudswell Clarke. Most had a somewhat chequered history of rebuilds, the Fox Walker, for example, built in 1875 was rebuilt by Avonside in 1903 and condemned on its visit to Swindon in 1923.

Several were actually sold off to collieries after amalgamation, living on for another thirty years or so.

All engines were originally named, not numbered, and one of the Hudswell Clarke locomotives, *Markland*, although only ten years old, was immediately condemned at Swindon in 1923, whilst her sister *Tarndune*, was 'Swindonised' with a new boiler and fittings.

The Hudswell Clarke saddle tank *Hilda* survived well, until 1954, in almost original condition; an extended bunker the only signs of alteration except, possibly, the safety valve cover, and the addition of a GWR number as well as her own name plate. *Hilda* was a feature of the Swansea Docks loco fleet, where she plied around the tracks complete with the typical dock warning bell.

The South Wales Mineral Railway (16) was associated with the GWR indirectly, from 1872, when it changed from broad to 'standard' gauge. The GWR involvement was to supply four saddle tanks of 645 class, constructed at Wolverhampton, as Swindon was still very much tied to the broad gauge at this time. All four had been disposed of by 1910, two sold for colliery use and two withdrawn.

Of the five locomotives handed over at the amalgamation, two were originally broad gauge saddle tanks from the Avonside Engine Company, built in 1873 for the South Devon Railway, and three were already GWR standard 1501 class locomotives purchased by the South Wales Mineral Railway about 1910. The two Avonside locos had already visited Swindon in 1910 when both received new boilers, and one of them was again rebuilt in 1924, receiving yet another boiler, and having its saddle tanks exchanged for the conventional pannier tanks of the GWR. 'Conventional' is not probably the right word for this period, but pannier tanks were to become conventional, with most saddle versions disappearing or being converted.

A little railway with a name seemingly from members of the Victorian Actors' Guild, the Cleobury Mortimer and Ditton Priors (17) had a 12-mile route for hauling granite from the Abdon Clee quarries. The standard gauge route took in about eight stopping places en route to the GWR Leominster to Kidderminster connection at Cleobury Mortimer.

Opened in 1908, the line had only two engines, little outside cylindered 0-6-0 saddle tanks by Manning Wardle, given the inevitable Swindon treatment of new boilers, cabs and pannier tanks on grouping. The passenger service disappeared in 1938 and the two engines were removed, one to the Gloucestershire/Worcestershire area and one to a Wrexham colliery. Both were withdrawn in the early 1950s.

An 'Addition' After the Grouping

Last but not least of the 'small fry' companies is one which came indirectly to the Great Western much later than those of the grouping, and more by default than design. To fill a gap in Great Western services, where certain towns were out on limbs, although basically served by the GWR trunk, 1885 saw the introduction of a 'steam tramway' to Weston-super-Mare, Clevedon and Portishead. The name changed in 1899 to 'Weston, Clevedon & Portishead Railway Company', the 14 track miles from Weston to Portishead Docks opening in 1907.

Two locomotives, Stroudley 'Terrier' tanks dating from 1875 and 1877 and originally on the London, Brighton & South Coast Railway, were among the assets taken over by the GWR when the line was closed in 1940, although quite successful in passenger traffic in the pre-war years. Having, as main creditors, acquired two engines, they were overhauled at Swindon in 1942 and set to work, one at Bristol and one in the Taunton area, the former until 1948, and the latter scrapped in 1954.

To Sum Up the Amalgamation

All in all, the grouping, as far as the Great Western was concerned, seemed to cause a great deal of work and reorganisation for little return. Although locomotives and track had been acquired, many of the locos were not wanted in the first place, and the little companies from which they came were in no way a 'threat' in commercial terms to the Great Western itself.

Had such 'threats' been apparent, the companies would have been added years before, in most cases, to the list of those taken over by the Great Western. As it was, it created more work at a period when there was already enough in the immediate post-war boom of getting things back on their feet again after a number of years of pressure and neglect caused by the First World War, although soon to change of course in the 'slump' years which followed.

The whole amalgamation may have put the other three main systems – the LMS, LNER and the SR – on their feet, but it really did nothing for the GWR, adding a great deal of responsibility for very little return.

It must be acknowledged, of course, that whilst the Great Western did not really want anything to do with the companies which were to be embraced by the 1921 Act, the feeling was mutual! The Welsh companies already felt they were really only 'feeders' to the Great Western system, being bottled in and doing all the 'dirty work' whilst the GWR creamed off all the best long routes and communication with the rest of the country. In any case many of the small railways were in financial terms doing very nicely, thank you!

It was this feeling of resentment, and knowing they were to lose their identities and individualities that contributed, in many cases, to the condition of the very decrepit stock that was handed over by some of them when the time came. The reasoning, which is quite understandable, must have been 'Why should we spend our resource cash on stock which will no longer be ours to control? If the Western wants it, let them carry the costs and pay for it!'

Thus stems the policy of 'running into the ground'. The Great Western repair, and particularly scrapping, programme on amalgamation shows how effective the 'running into the ground' policy actually was!

By the time of the amalgamation, however, the high profitability days of the companies were nominally over. No longer was the British High Seas Fleet powered solely by coal, and those remaining vessels would be converted or replaced in the near future. The fleets were reducing, both Royal and Mercantile, the world over, and oil was becoming the fuel in demand. Industrial patterns themselves were soon to change.

The 50 million tonnes of coal, which had been the average per year during the First World War, reduced drastically as demand fell quite rapidly after the conflict. The boom years of coal, and the fame of the Welsh railways which handled the immense tonnages, were over. For the Great Western, the grouping was imposed too late.

After the Amalgamation

From the Amalgamation of 1922 came a quarter of a century of consolidation, interrupted by the advent of the Second World War when everything was once again overworked as in the previous conflict. Immediately following the war a major general election upheaval occurred, the new policies including a momentous railway change which had been mooted for many years, and fudged over by the amalgamation itself. 'Nationalisation' had arrived, and the Great Western Railway disappeared under the title of British Railways (Western Region).

Handling the additional 1,000 or so locomotives from the amalgamation had been more of a nuisance value to the GWR, and as the examinations, rebuilding and scrappings of the various locomotives took place, so design and building activity flourished for bigger and better Great Western engines.

Delayed somewhat by the exigencies of the first international conflict, the progress of design from the four-cylinder Stars and two-cylinder Saints had blossomed into a new, more powerful design, emerging as the 'Castle' class in 1923. In the following year, the first British 4-6-2 'Pacific' type locomotive, 'The Great Bear', was rebuilt as a Castle class, having survived on an experimental but restricted basis, from its construction date in 1906.

Design progressed, and in 1927 the pride of the Great Western, the 'King' class, emerged from the Swindon Shops. However successful, the class was limited to thirty only, whilst the forerunner 'Castle' class design was continued right into the early years of Nationalisation and the birth of the 'Standard' locomotives.

The only 'new' passenger locomotive to emerge during these years was the two-cylinder 'County' or '1000' class, and when all is considered, actual locomotive 'design' as such stopped with Churchward. All subsequent passenger locos designed by his successors were, in literary terms, plagiarisms of Churchward's designs – a little larger here, slightly altered there, but really Churchward based, and in effect the history of the broad gauge locomotives repeated.

The complete departure, attempted by Hawkesworth in Great Western design, the 1500 class pannier tank 0-6-0 with outside cylinders and Walshaert valve gear, broke the mould of Churchward, but came too late in what must have been a very frustrating period for the last 'CM&EE' of the Great Western Railway.

Thus, with 'Nationalisation' in 1947 came the end of independence of the Great Western Railway. All the struggles with canals, plateways, tramroads and other railway companies now confined to the history books and the memories of the reducing numbers who knew the Great Western Railway as it was at the height of the steam years.

Its place has been secured in railway history.

Great Western Development and Growth – Constituent Companies

Second List and Map – 1926

The Map came at a time of the final major expansion of the Great Western Railway on the establishment of the 'Big Four'. It details the final identity of the various Constituent Companies at this late period after all the changes and machinations of the previous hundred years. This is a large map. The following pages show close-up views of each section and a spread of the map in its entirety.

The list which follows has two columns: one shows the 'ALPHA' number, which refers to the alphabetical first list reference; the second column to the companies shown on the comprehensive map of 1926 following. By the date of the map (1926) lines had been initiated by the GWR and others combined.

Constituent & Allied Railway Companies Absorbed by GWR

Alpha No.	Map Order	Companies		Alpha No.	Map Order	Companies
132	1	Great Western Railway		49	21	Bristol Harbour Extension
	2	Hammersmith & City		54	22	Bristol & South Wales Union
332	3	Birmingham, Bristol & Thames Junction		52	23	Bristol Port Railway & Pier
331	4	West London (Extension)		17	24	Avonmouth & Severn Tunnel Junction (GW)
	5	South Lambert Goods Branch (GW)		15	25	Avonmouth & Filton (GW))
	6	Ealing & Shepherds Bush (GW)			26	South Wales & Bristol Direct (GWR)
131	7	Great Western & Brentford		46	27	Bristol & Exeter (Ex-Taw Vale Railway)
134	8	Great Western & Uxbridge		70	28	Chard & Taunton
286	9	Staines & West Drayton		72	29	Cheddar Valley & Yatton
7	10	Acton & Wycombe		116	30	Exe Valley
316	11	Uxbridge & Denham (GW)		51	31	Bristol & Portishead Pier & Railway
135	12	Wycombe		100	32	Devon & Somerset
130	13	Great Marlow		185	33	Minehead
325	14	Watlington & Princes Risborough		336	34	West Somerset
				350	35	Wrington Vale Light
324	15	Wallingford & Watlington		91	36	Culm Valley Light
119	16	Faringdon		309	37	Tiverton & North Devon
299	17	Swindon & Highworth		25	38	Berkshire & Hampshire
175	18	Malmesbury		24	39	Berkshire & Hampshire Extension
60	19	Calne			40	Coley Branch – Reading (GW)
48	20	Bristol Harbour				

101	41	Didcot, Newbury & Southampton Junction	237	72	Plymouth & Great Western Dock
149	42	Lambourn Valley	83	73	Cornwall
182	43	Midland South Western Junction	158	74	Liskeard & Caradon
300	44	Swindon, Marlborough & Andover	159	75	Liskeard & Looe Union Canal
178	45	Marlborough & Grafton (see also 43)		76	Bodmin (GWR)
308	46	Tidworth Camp (War Dept worked line)	84	77	Cornwall Minerals
			214	78	Newquay & Cornwall Junction
177	47	Marlborough	170	79	Lostwithiel & Fowey
287	48	Stert & Westbury (GW)	313	80	Trenance Valley (GWR)
340	49	Wilts, Somerset & Weymouth	254	81	Retew Branch Extension (GWR)
63	50	Camerton & Limpley Stoke (GWR)	315	82	Truro & Newquay (GWR)
50	51	Bristol & North Somerset	330	83	West Cornwall
107	52	East Somerset	140	84	Hayle
67	53	Castle Cary & Langport (GWR)	142	85	Helston
152	54	Langport & Durston (GWR)	290	86	St Ives Branch
44	55	Bridport		87	Oxford
1	56	Abbotsbury	6	88	Abingdon
335	57	Weymouth & Portland	227	89	Oxford & Rugby
9	58	Admiralty Line (Portland) (GW&LSW Jt)	341	90	Witney
			106	91	East Gloucestershire
105	59	Easton & Church Hope	343	92	Woodstock
58	60	South Devon (see 153 ALPHA	12	93	Aynho & Ashendon (GWR)
	61	Dartmouth & Torbay	251	94	Princes Risborough & Grendon Underwood
	62	Launceston & South Devon			
281	63	South Devon & Tavistock	32	95	Birmingham & Oxford Junction
201	64	Moreton Hampstead & South Devon	293	96	Stratford-on-Avon
	65	Buckfastleigh, Totnes & South Devon	30	97	Birmingham & Henley-in-Arden
	66	Exeter, Teign Valley & Chagford	31	98	Birmingham, Warws & Stratford-on-Avon
305	67	Teign Valley	8	99	Alcester
310	68	Torbay & Brixham		100	Birmingham, Wolverhampton & Dudley
148	69	Kingsbridge & Salcombe	272	101	Shrewsbury & Birmingham
235	70	Princetown	326	102	Wellington & Drayton
353	71	South Hams Extension (see Yealmpton Railway)	205	103	Nantwich & Market Drayton
			273	104	Shrewsbury, Chester & Oswestry Junction

218	105	North Wales Mineral	78	136	Cleobury Mortimer & Ditton Priors
318	106	Vale of Llangollen	203	137	Much Wenlock & Severn Junction
164	107	Llangollen & Corwen	329	138	Wenlock
87	108	Corwen & Bala	157	139	Lightmoor & Coalbrookdale (GWR)
19	109	Bala & Dolgelley			
20	110	Bala & Festiniog	327	140	Wellington & Severn Junction
121	111	Festiniog & Glaeno			
245	112	Pontycysyllte (Stratford & Moreton)	73	141	Cheltenham & Great Western Union
96	113	Denbighshire Railways (GWR)		142	Tetbury Branch (GWR)
			75	143	Cheltenham & Honeybourne (GWR)
239	114	Ponkey Branch Railway (GWR)	126	144	Gloucester & Dean Forest
347	115	Ponkey Branch (GWR) (Wrexham & Min)	264	145	Ross & Ledbury
				146	Newent
349	116	Wrexham & Mineral Extension	145	147	Hereford, Ross & Gloucester
204	117	Moss Valley (GWR)	265	148	Ross & Monmouth
76	118	Chester & Birkenhead	81	149	Coleford, Monmouth, Usk & Pontypool
	119	Chester, Lancs & Cheshire Junction	200	150	Wye Valley
27	120	Birkenhead	82	151	Coleford
228	121	Oxford, Worcs & Wolverhampton	127	152	Golden Valley
			274	153	Shrewsbury & Hereford
333	122	Worcester & Hereford	275	154	Leominster & Bromyard
211	123	Newport, Abergavenny & Hereford	156	155	Leominster & Kington
			147	156	Kington & Eardisley
36	124	Bourton-on-the-Water	307	157	Tenbury
21	125	Banbury & Cheltenham Direct	172	158	Ludlow & Clee Hill
			277	159	Shrewsbury & Welshpool
291	126	Shipston-on-Stour (Ex-Stratford & Moreton)	61	160	Oswestry, Ellesmere & Whitchurch
344	127	Worcester, Bromyard & Leominster	61	161	Owestry & Newtown
			61	162	Llanidloes & Newtown
	128	Stourbridge Town Branch (GWR)	61	163	Newtown & Machynlleth
289	129	Stourbridge	5	164	Aberystwyth & Welsh Coast (and 166)
223	130	Dudley & Oldbury Junction	61	165	Mid Wales
138	131	Halesowen Branch (Netherton) (GWR)	348	166	Cambrian (160, 161, 162, 163, 164, & 165)
137	132	Halesowen & Bromsgrove			
45	133	Bridgnorth & Wolverhampton (GWR)		167	Tanat Valley Light
268	134	Severn Valley	275	168	Potteries, Shrewsbury & North Wales
306	135	Tenbury & Bewdley			

328	169	Welshpool & Llanfair Light
	170	Van
179	171	Mawddwy
320	172	Vale of Rheidol
176	173	Manchester & Milford
150	174	Lampeter, Aberayron & Newquay Light
284	175	South Wales
123	176	Bullo (see also Forest of Dean Railway)
181	177	Mitcheldean Road & Forest of Dean Junction
123	178	Forest of Dean Central
173	179	Lydney & Lidbrook (Severn & Wye Railway&Can)
270	180	Severn Bridge (Severn & Wye)
125	181	Gloucester & Berkeley Docks Branch (MR)
	182	Severn Tunnel
108	183	East Usk
240	184	Pontypool, Caerleon & Newport
186	185	Monmouthshire Railway & Canal
230	186	Neutral Mile (Park Mile Railway)
141	187	Abercarn (Halls or Llanover Tram Road)
59	188	Brynmawr & Western Valleys
10	189	Alexandra Dock & Railway
246	190	Pontypridd, Caerphilly & Newport
266	191	Rumney
41	192	Brecon & Merthyr Tydfil Junction
263	193	Roath Dock Branch (GWR)
258	194	Riverside Branch (Cardiff) (GWR)
57	195	But Docks (see also Cardiff Railway)
259	196	Rhymney
260	197	Rhymney & LNWR Joint
302	198	Taff Bargoed Joint (GW & Rhymney)
253	199	Quakers Yard & Merthyr Joint (GW & Rhymney)
303	200	Taff Vale
133	201	Great Western & Taff Vale Joint
3	202	Aberdare
94	203	Dare Valley
257	204	Rhonda Valley & Hirwain Junction
312	205	Treferig Valley
166	206	Llantrisant & Taff Vale Junction
90	207	Cowbridge
89	208	Cowbridge & Aberthaw
65	209	Cardiff, Penarth & Barry Junction
233	210	Penarth, Harbour, Dock & Railway
232	211	Penarth Extension
23	212	Barry Docks & Railway
317	213	Vale of Glamorgan
111	214	Ely Valley
110	215	Ely & Clydach Valleys
103	216	Duffryn, Llynvi & Porthcawl
169	217	Llynvi Valley
112	218	Ely Valley Extension
221	219	Ogmore Valley
64	220	Cardiff & Ogmore Valley
	221	Llynvi & Ogmore (see also 216)
249	222	Port Talbot Railway & Docks
283	223	South Wales Mineral
256	224	Rhondda & Swansea Bay
55	225	Briton Ferry, Dock & Railway
296	226	Vale of Neath
4	227	Aberdare Valley
296	228	Swansea & Neath
295	229	Swansea Harbour
297	230	Swansea Vale, Neath & Brecon Junction
104	231	Dulas Valley Mineral (see Neath & Brecon)

	232	Swansea District (GWR)
295	233	Swansea Harbour Trust
202	234	Morriston (GWR)
92	235	Clydach, Pontardawe & Cwmgorse (GWR)
163	236	Llanelly Railway & Dock
322	237	Valley of Towey
162	238	Llanelly & Mynydd Mawr
56	239	Burry Port Co. (see also 240)
136	240	Gwendraeth Valleys Railway
62	241	Carmarthen & Cardigan (see 240)

	231	242	Pembroke & Tenby
337	243	Whitland & Cardigan
206	244	Maenclochog (& Narberth Road Railway)
217	245	North Pembrokeshire & Fishguard
77	246	Clarbeston Road & Letterston (GWR)
122	247	Fishguard, Rosslare Railways & Harbours
184	248	Milford
323	249	Victoria Station & Pimlico

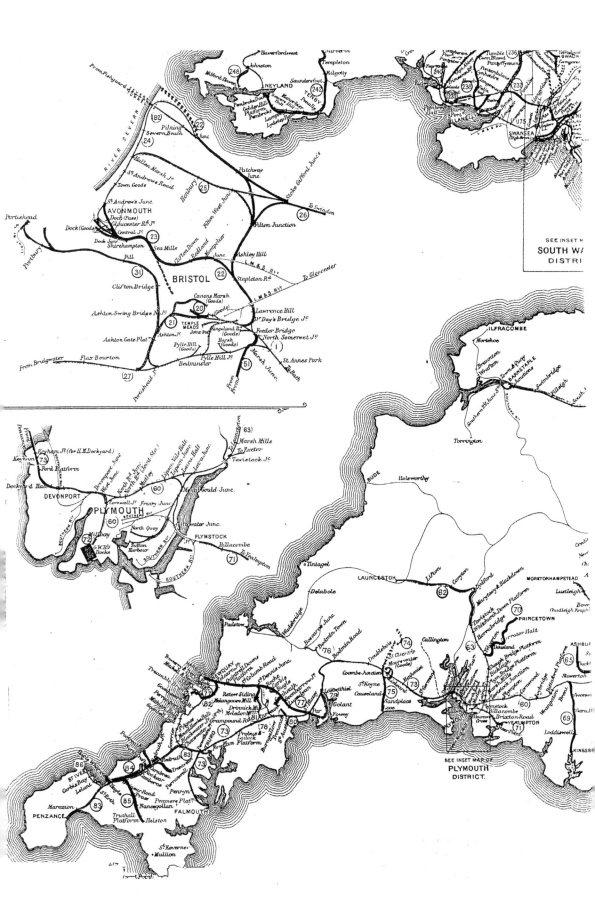

GREAT·WESTERN·RAILW

SCALE·8 MILES TO AN INCH.

DECEMBER, 1926.

Explanation.

Great Western Lines	shewn thus
Foreign Lines	"
Joint	"
Authorised Lines and Lines in course of construction	"
Lines Closed or Abandoned	++++++++

LITHOGRAPHED BY W. & A.K. JOHNSTON, LIMITED, EDINBURGH.

WESTERN RAILWAY.

E·8 MILES TO AN INCH.

DECEMBER, 1926.

Explanation.

Western Lines shown thus
r Lines
rised Lines and Lines
rse of construction
Closed or Abandoned

LITHOGRAPHED BY W. & A.K. JOHNSTON, LIMITED, EDINBURGH.

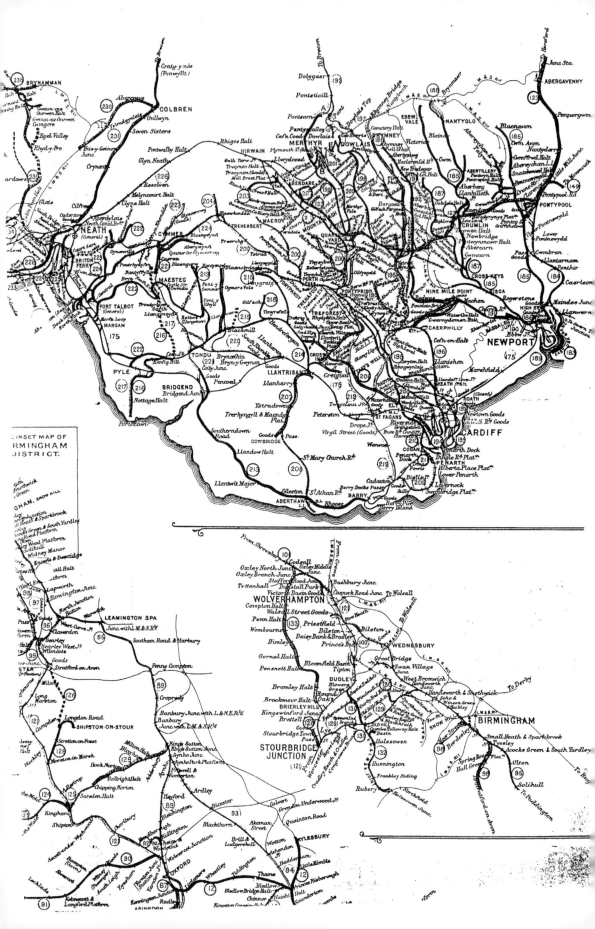

Tail Piece

Whilst the all-powerful Great Western Railway dominated the transport scene, the many canal, tramroad, plateway and small railway companies became objects of industrial archaeology and historical interest. Many canal routes and branch line railways had become grass and weed grown tracks through the fields, possibly flanked by rows of trees and hedges. Some rail beds were now cycle tracks and paved walks, maybe with a commemorative plaque attached to a boulder to explain what had been there in the past.

This situation began to change, albeit very slowly, with the first enthusiasts taking over a short length of branch line bed with the intention of running a steam locomotive on it once again, after relaying a length of second-hand track, which itself had probably lain in a weed grown pile for a number of years. So from the tentative start the small railway companies have returned, now run mostly by volunteers and enthusiasts, in many cases having to start the company literally from scratch, negotiating land agreements with local councils and doing everything the pioneer entrepreneurs had done originally.

From the 1980s, the interest in the many abandoned canal routes has also expanded, with volunteers seeking grants and working hard to open up long abandoned waterways, still shown on the Ordnance Survey maps, but with a recognizable overgrown length now suddenly terminating in a flat cultivated field, the clay lined canal bed long buried.

The closure of many mining and quarrying complexes has also triggered ideas of refurbishing for the tourist market. The Morwhellam Quay complex has already been mentioned, and the resurrection of the tramway into the mine is another step forward, as well as back in time, to the recognition of the part played by the plateways and tramroads in the development of transport generally. (As a historical feature, who will be first to initiate a replica plateway on stone blocks?)

The Great Western Railway, as known to many, has long gone and been replaced by a system which Brunel would have rejected out of hand. For the way to run a railway, the powers-that-be could well take a leaf out of the books of the small companies now busily and effectively resurrecting a past which actually worked! One company, one chairman, of one board that controls all aspects of the projects; where, in modern phraseology, 'the buck stops'.

Let us give the rebuilders of lengths of canal, tramroad, plateway and branch line our full support. They are doing a good job!

A railway official publication lists 365 companies with a finger in the Great Western Railway pie!* Where is there a modern-day Brunel who could take us back to where this book started. To the absorbing or elimination of all companies by the developing Great Western Railway – to replace the current chaos!

---

* 'Rail-news' Directory 2002 and subsequent dates. Editorial: Rail-news, East Side Offices, Kings Cross Station, London N1 9AP

A Note on Bibliography and Source Material

This little outline work of the rise and fall of the south-western transport systems of Britain both before and during the 'rise and rise' of the Great Western Railway, has been compiled from many sources, a combination of canal, plateway, tramroad, and railway histories, including nineteenth-century engineering magazines, advertisements and newspapers and GWR archive material. There are general works listing problems, solutions and development of canals and plateways, specific works dealing in detail with virtually any and every major canal and railway you wish to name. Biographies of boat people who sailed, maintained, owned, lived on, or exploited the canals abound. The same applies to tramroad, plateway and railway subjects. Acts of Parliament, pamphlets, Records of the Institute of Civil Engineers. Transactions of the Newcomen Society, period details from local newspaper files, records of specific interest from the British Transport Historical Records collection (stored at the Public Records Office), and records in local reference libraries. Parliamentary debates recorded in issues of Hansard make very interesting and incisive reading, and etc.

There are also many magazines in existence dealing with all transport subjects, both historical and modern. The transport history of Britain is probably one of the most detailed and recorded subjects, with such a vast range of individual possible studies which are subjects by themselves. There are also the preservationist groups, re-establishing old transport routes in many areas. Most are volunteers. Whilst there are modern works which detail the history and current standing of many canals, Joseph Priestley's work of 1831 (reprinted by David & Charles in 1969), will give early details of every canal and river navigation in the country, highlighting all details such as costs of construction and subsequent tolls and duties for its use. Also included will be found details of the Acts authorising the navigation, and construction details, length, number of locks etc. Truly a monumental work of the period which includes reference to early tramroads associated with the various undertakings.

The choices for further study are thus vast, so if this little book has triggered an interest in a particular aspect of transport, there is, somewhere, the information you seek.

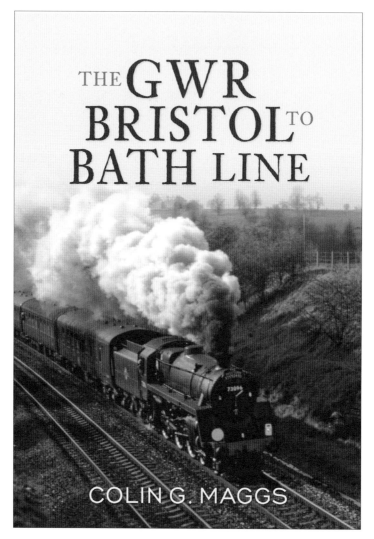

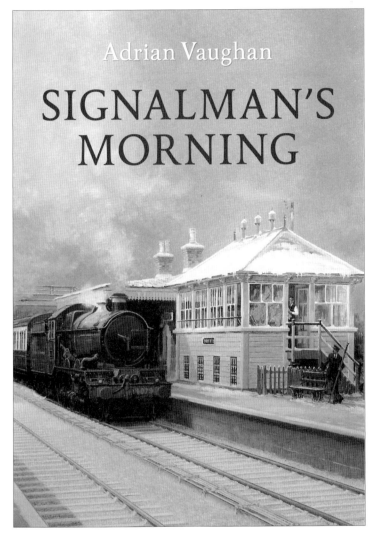

Signalman's Morning

Adrian Vaughan

The first book in Adrian Vaughan's Signalman's trilogy. A classic of railway literature.

978 1 4456 0256 1

190 pages, 50 b&w illustrations

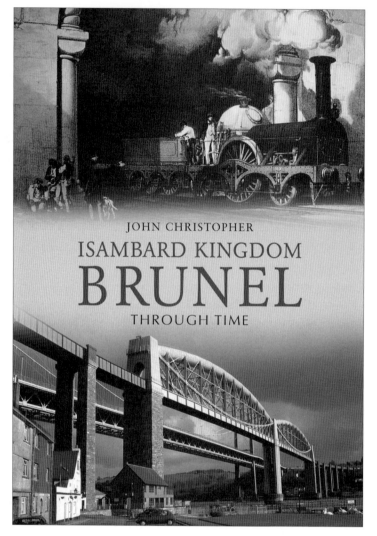